SHAKING HEAVEN & EARTH
THE TSUNAMI EARTHQUAKE PROPHECIES

LYLE K. NORTON

Outskirts Press, Inc.
Denver, Colorado

The opinions expressed in this manuscript are solely the opinions of the author and do not represent the opinions or thoughts of the publisher. The author represents and warrants that s/he either owns or has the legal right to publish all material in this book.

Shaking Heaven & Earth
The Tsunami Earthquake Prophecies
All Rights Reserved.
Copyright © 2008 Lyle K. Norton
v2.0

This book may not be reproduced, transmitted, or stored in whole or in part by any means, including graphic, electronic, or mechanical without the express written consent of the publisher except in the case of brief quotations embodied in critical articles and reviews.

Outskirts Press, Inc.
http://www.outskirtspress.com

ISBN: 978-1-4327-2766-6

Library of Congress Control Number: 2008931571

Outskirts Press and the "OP" logo are trademarks belonging to Outskirts Press, Inc.

PRINTED IN THE UNITED STATES OF AMERICA

DEDICATION

This book is dedicated to my wife, Hati. She started me on this journey when she asked me to find out about the space explosion she heard about on the news. She encouraged me in my study, put up with my long hours on the computer, and persevered through it all.

Thank you, Hati.

CONTENTS

Section 1:	The Events	1
Chapter 1	The Tsunami Earthquake	3
Chapter 2	The Starquake	9
Chapter 3	The Space Fire	15
Section 2:	The Prophecies	19
Chapter 4	Current Prophecy	21
Chapter 5	Previous Prophecy	29
Chapter 6	Last Day Prophecy	33
Chapter 7	The Two Laws	39
Chapter 8	The Sanctuary	49
Chapter 9	The Day of Atonement	75
Chapter 10	Earthquakes	83
Chapter 11	Vision of Dry Bones	99
Chapter 12	Glory	107
Chapter 13	The Sealing & Probation	113
Chapter 14	The Elijah Message	119

INTRODUCTION

What is prophecy? Is it just history in advance? Why would God tell us history in advance? Can't we just wait until it happens? Or is there something more involved in prophecy than just history? Why is it important to me? Is there a revealing of the secrets of God? Where are we in time? Are we really near the end of time? What does it all mean? I hope that after reading this book you are better able to answer all of these questions.

This may be the most important book you read in this decade (other than the Bible). Not because it is a great literary work or a masterfully written story, but because it reveals the secrets of God and where we are in time. Knowing where we are in time may cause you to change your priorities. Present truth has a way of doing that.

The deeper meaning behind prophetic events is what this book intends to explore. This book is not intended to be scientifically exhaustive or to tell you everything you need to know about God. There are other books and the Bible for those purposes. The intent of this book is to look at current end time prophecy and give the reader reference points to build on in their personal study of prophecy and the Bible. It is the hope of the author that the reader will be awakened to the deeper meaning of prophecy that I believe we should all seek to understand. I invite you to take this exploration with me now. Time is, after all, running out.

Many have asked are there really specific prophecies about the Tsunami earthquake? Are there specific prophecies, in our time, that tell us something more than just that an event happened? What does prophecy really tell us? Why would God tell us about specific events? Read on to find the answers to these and many other questions. You will be amazed at what God is revealing through prophecy.

THE EVENTS

CHAPTER 1
THE TSUNAMI EARTHQUAKE

On December 26, 2004 at 00:58:53 UTC (Universal Coordinated Time), the second largest seismograph recorded earthquake struck. This earthquake caused a series of devastating tsunamis that spread throughout the Indian Ocean. It bowed the Earth like a gigantic cello string and the entire planet vibrated more than ½ inch and wobbled on its axis by more than 1 inch. The North Pole moved and is now approximately one inch from its previous location. The 2004 Indian Ocean earthquake (also called the Asian Tsunami, Boxing Day Tsunami or just The Tsunami Earthquake) was an undersea earthquake with its epicenter off the west coast of Sumatra, Indonesia. What caused this earthquake to be so devastating?

Earthquakes are classified on the Richter scale by their largest-amplitude seismic wave. These seismic waves come in longer or shorter periods, or wavelengths; but only the most powerful quakes have very much energy in long-period waves. Seismologists initially used seismic waves with periods of about 300 seconds to set the magnitude of the Sumatran earthquake at 9.0, placing it as the fifth most powerful event on record.

Seismologists Seth Stein and Emile Okal at Northwestern University in Evanston, Illinois, studied seismograms taken from 7 stations around the world in the week following the earthquake. They looked for the longest-period waves possible, those lasting about 3200 seconds (53 minutes). This is the lowest frequency of the planet and is called the fundamental frequency. What they found was the longest duration of faulting ever recorded. "We found, to our surprise, that there was three times more energy out there than at the 300-second period," Stein said. "It was colossal." This reclassified the earthquake on the logarithmic Richter scale to magnitude 9.3, second only to the 9.5 magnitude quake recorded in Chile in 1960. However, the tsunami earthquake was of longer duration.

Let me try to put the energy of this earthquake in different terms for you so that you may be better able to relate to it. The power of this earthquake was equivalent to 23,000 Hiroshima size atomic bombs. Multiply the atomic bomb times 23,000! It was greater than the power of all the earthquakes in the previous 5 years added together. Even with these images in our minds it is difficult for us to grasp the enormity of the power of this event.

The general shape of the Earth is slightly oblong, making it about 26 miles wider at the equator than between the poles. This 9.3 magnitude earthquake actually altered the shape of the earth. Calculations have estimated that this catastrophic land displacement caused a small reduction in the bulge, making the planet more round. "The waistline was reduced by not quite a millimeter because of the earthquake," said Benjamin Fong Chao from NASA's Goddard Space Flight Center. This slimming down sped up the rotation of the Earth, much like when a spinning ice skater pulls in their arms to increase their speed. The length of the day accordingly decreased by 2.68 millionths of a second. In a unique sense, time was shortened.

An 800 mile section of fault line moved and slipped, thrusting upward from 33 to 50 feet vertically. The coast of Sumatra moved as much as 9.8 feet, and the north end of Simeulue Island moved 6.6 feet. The whole planet vibrated and wobbled on its axis by 1 inch. Many smaller earthquakes occurred along with this earthquake all over the planet, one as far away as Alaska. You'll understand why after I explain the event that occurred simultaneously.

The tsunami that was produced from this quake devastated the shores of Indonesia, Sri Lanka, India, Thailand and other countries with waves of over 100 feet high in some places. An eyewitness stated that the wave he saw was taller than the highest palm tree. These waves moved across the ocean at approximately 500 mph. As they reached the shallower waters of the coastline they slowed and began to stack up in height. It caused serious damage and deaths as far as the east coast of Africa, with the furthest recorded death due to the tsunami occurring at Port Elizabeth in South Africa, 5,000 miles away from the epicenter.

Tsunamis are unlike wind-generated waves, which many of us may have observed on a local lake or at a coastal beach, in that they are characterized as shallow-water waves, with long periods and wave lengths. The wind-generated swell that is seen at a California beach because of a storm out in the Pacific comes rhythmically rolling in, one wave after another, and might have a period of about 10 seconds and a wave length from trough to trough of 150 yards. A tsunami, on the other hand, can have a wavelength in excess of 60 miles and a period on the order of an hour.

For those of you who are into science and like the details and particulars, let's go through the anatomy of these waves. Because of their long wave lengths, tsunamis behave as shallow-water waves. A wave becomes a shallow-water wave when the ratio between the water depth and its wave length gets very small. Shallow-water waves move at a speed that is equal to the square root of the product of the acceleration of gravity (9.8 m/s/s) and the water depth. In the Pacific Ocean, where the typical water depth is about 20,000 feet deep, a tsunami travels at approximately 550 miles per hour. Because the rate at which a wave loses its energy is inversely related to its wave length, tsunamis not only propagate at high speeds, they can also travel great, transoceanic distances with limited energy losses.

As the tsunami reaches more shallow water the shape of the wave changes and slows because of the frictional forces of the ocean floor and can build to great height because of the incredible volume of water.

What does all of this mean in terms of this tsunami earthquake? Because the waves slow down near the shore, the water behind the leading edge "catches up" and creates an even more massive wave. When the tsunami waves of this earthquake hit the shore they were miles long behind the leading edge of the wave. I have seen a video of one of the waves rushing across the land near Banda Aceh, Indonesia. It was still approximately 15 feet high at 3 miles inland and there was no end to the wave in sight. Some of the waves reached more than 5 miles inland. The devastation was incomprehensible. This earthquake is the largest earthquake, in terms of loss of life and devastation, in modern times. It may never be known exactly how many lives were lost because of incomplete records in very remote places. The best estimate I can find is that more than 288,608 people perished and more than 42,883 are missing. In other words, more than 331,491 people are gone.

CHAPTER 2
THE STARQUAKE

Just 44.6 hours after the Tsunami earthquake, gamma ray telescopes orbiting the Earth picked up the arrival of the brightest gamma ray burst ever recorded! A huge starquake halfway across the galaxy had so much power the gamma rays briefly altered Earth's upper atmosphere on December 27, 2004 at 21 hours 36 minutes UTC (Universal Time). No known eruption beyond our solar system has ever appeared as bright upon arrival. This starquake originated approximately 47,000 light-years away.

The gamma ray blast was 150 times more intense than any burst that had been previously recorded, equaling the brightness of the full Moon, but radiating most of its electrical energy at gamma ray wavelengths which are not visible to the naked eye. Gamma ray counts spiked to a maximum in 1.5 seconds and then declined over a 5 minute period with 7.57 second pulsations. The blast temporarily changed the shape the Earth's ionosphere, distorting the transmission of long-wavelength radio signals.

The flash, an electromagnetic pulse, came from a special variety of neutron star known as a magnetar. "Had this happened within 10 light-years of us, it would have severely damaged our atmosphere and possibly have triggered a mass extinction," said Bryan Gaensler of the Harvard-Smithsonian Center for Astrophysics (CfA). "This is a once-in-a-lifetime event," said Rob Fender of Southampton University in the UK. "We have observed an object only 20 kilometers across [12 miles], on the other side of our galaxy, releasing more energy in a tenth of a second than the Sun emits in 100,000 years."

After gaining more data scientists are now saying that this is inaccurate. The 1/10 of a second release was actually equivalent to 150,000 years of our sun's energy release. Further, that during the first 200 ms, or 2/10 of a second, the amount of energy released was equivalent to what our Sun would radiate in 250,000 years! According to all known science it is impossible for a star of this size to release that much energy. The closest any computer model could come using the laws of physics, was 150 times less. And even that model significantly slowed the stars rotation as is consistent with the laws of physics, which did not occur.

When any significant amount of energy is released from a starquake, the spin is slowed. To put it another way, every action has an equal and opposite reaction. Not only did the star not slow, it released 150 times more energy than was scientifically possible. Researchers can't explain why the burst was so incredible. In order to explain the magnitude of this event some scientists have suggested that the star is much closer than previously thought. There has been significant research done with triangulation from satellite that refutes that suggestion. There is good evidence that the distance to the star is correct.

This star, SGR 1806-20 spins once in only 7.57 seconds and is still rotating at the same speed. Why did the December event not result in any slowing of its spin rate, as every other event like this has? For over a 10th of a second, it was brighter than a full Moon, and briefly overwhelmed delicate sensors.

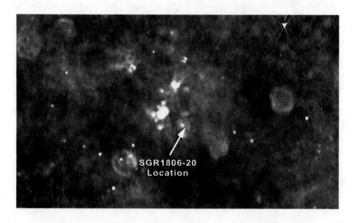

The flare on SGR 1806-20 unleashed about 15,000 trillion trillion trillion watts of power, that's 1.5 X 10 to the 39th power or a 15 with 39 zeros after it.

"The next biggest flare ever seen from any soft gamma repeater was peanuts compared to this incredible December event," said Gaensler of the CfA. This second event is physically impossible according to scientific law.

But this is not the most amazing part of this event. What hasn't been widely known is that preceding the gamma ray burst a longitudinal gravity wave of incredible power reached the earth. This gravity wave preceded the gamma burst by 44.6 hours and struck the earth causing the Tsunami earthquake.

SHAKING HEAVEN & EARTH

Astronomers have theorized that gamma ray bursts travel in association with gravity wave bursts for many years. Experiments carried out by Eugene Podkletnov show that a shock front outburst produces a longitudinal gravitational wave that travels forward faster than the burst. He has found that this gravity wave pulse has a speed in excess of 64 times the speed of light. Observations suggest that the gravity wave decreases its superluminal speed and eventually slows to the speed of light as the shock front expands. But meanwhile, the gravity wave will have obtained a significant head start over the electromagnetic wave radiation component traveling in its wake (light waves, gamma rays, etc.). So the gravity wave from such an outburst (and its resultant earthquake activity) would precede the gamma ray burst component. The fact that the earthquake was 44.6 hours ahead of the gamma ray burst correlates with this data perfectly. Now you also know why there were many other earthquakes all over the earth.

The entire solar system was shaking from the event; in fact, the entire galaxy was experiencing a kind of gravitational vibration or ringing as this wave propagated. "This explosion was akin to hitting the neutron star with a gigantic hammer, causing it to ring like a bell," said Richard Rothschild, an astrophysicist at the University of California's Center for Astrophysics and Space Sciences. "Now the question is, what does the frequency of the neutron star's oscillations—the tone produced by the ringing bell—mean?" The quakes ripped through the neutron star at an incredible speed, vibrating the star at 94.5 cycles per second. "This is near the frequency of the 22nd key of a piano, F sharp," said Tomaso Belloni, an Italian member of the team who measured the signals. Not only did our whole solar system ring with the sound of this bell but the whole galaxy rang with the sound of the bell.

An interesting aside is that bell frequencies are assigned numbers according to their frequency. The number that is assigned to the F sharp closest to this F sharp (one octave above as there is no assignment for a frequency this low) is 7, which is often associated as God's number. In Revelation alone there are 7 churches, 7 Spirits, 7 candlesticks, 7 stars, 7 seals, 7 horns, 7 eyes, 7 angels, 7 trumpets, 7 thunders, 7 vials, and 7 last plagues.

So, what does all of this mean? It means that the Tsunami Earthquake was caused by the starquake and both are beyond the limits of science and did not happen by chance. However, it doesn't stop there. The event in the next chapter is even more incredible.

CHAPTER 3
THE SPACE FIRE

Just prior to the starquake and tsunami earthquake, US scientists detected the most massive space explosion and fire ever observed. This space fire was discovered by using NASA's orbiting Chandra X-ray Observatory which is controlled from a base in Cambridge, Massachusetts. Brian McNamara and his colleagues made this discovery. The location of the fire is in deep space approximately 2.6 billion light years away. The galaxy cluster is called MS 0735.6+7421. The amount of energy released by this fire, equivalent to 300 million of our suns, is baffling scientists the world over.

The gaseous smoke cloud emitted from this fire has a diameter of 1.3 million light years and equals the mass of a trillion suns, more than the mass of all the stars in our Milky Way Galaxy. By the way, a light year is approximately 5.8 trillion miles, so if you wish to know the diameter in miles, multiply that times 1.3 million. That is a really big number.

One scientist is quoted as saying, "This is bigger than what we thought the big bang was." Now that has to be really big. The big bang theory is that all the mass of the universe was in one place at one time and that the mass was so great it attracted all the gases in the universe and something lit a match. Then, presto, the big bang. The point is that according to the laws of physics, it requires all the mass of the universe, in terms of gravitational pull, to draw this much fuel or gas into one place in order to have this large of an explosion or fire. And we know that all the mass of the universe is not located in that area of space, don't we?

"The interesting issue is, what is the source of the fuel in this case?" said Paul Nulsen of the Harvard-Smithsonian Center of Astrophysics. Interesting is a gross understatement, impossible would be more scientifically accurate.

Let me give you an example of what this fire is like. Let's say we parked a tanker truck filled with gasoline at the center of the United States and lit it on fire. The fire, instead of just burning in a city block area, burns across the whole United States and the smoke cloud encompasses the sun and the moon. But, you say, there isn't enough fuel to make a fire that big, precisely. This fire is burning without any possible explanation for the amount of fuel necessary to have a fire of this magnitude and duration.

I'd like you to think about the incredible magnitude of this fire with a seemingly never ending source of fuel. What this means is that this fire can only be compared with the burning bush that didn't burn up. It is physically impossible. As Moses turned aside and considered this strange fire that didn't burn the bush up (see Exodus chapter 3), we need to turn aside and consider this incredible fire that is physically impossible. When God showed the burning bush to Moses He was about to deliver His people. Is He about to deliver His people again? Is it almost time to go to the Promised Land?

THE PROPHECIES

CHAPTER 4
CURRENT PROPHECY

God tells us in Amos 3:7, "Surely the Lord GOD will do nothing, but he revealeth his secret unto his servants the prophets." So, if there is a spiritual significance to these events, it must be in prophecy. Notice in this scripture that God is revealing His secret. In other words, the purpose of prophecy is to reveal something about God, what He is doing, or something He has done that has relevance to us. God doesn't tell us anything that we don't need to know. However, He does tell us His secrets, which are very personal and important to Him and to us.

We need to consider the characteristics of these three events: fire and smoke, a starquake, and an earthquake. Are there any prophecies that have all these characteristics in them? Let's go to the Bible.

David said prophetically in 2 Samuel 22:7-16, "In my distress I called upon the LORD, and cried to my God: and he did hear my voice out of his temple, and my cry did enter into his ears. 8Then the earth shook and trembled; the foundations of heaven moved and shook, because he was wroth. 9There went up a smoke out of his nostrils, and fire out of his mouth devoured: coals were kindled by it. 10He bowed the heavens also, and came down; and darkness was under his feet. 11And he rode upon a cherub, and did fly: and he was seen upon the wings of the wind. 12And he made darkness pavilions round about him, dark waters, and thick clouds of the skies. 13Through the brightness before him were coals of fire kindled. 14The LORD thundered from heaven, and the most High uttered his voice. 15And he sent out arrows, and scattered them; lightning, and discomfited them. 16And the channels of the sea appeared, the foundations of the world were discovered, at the rebuking of the LORD, at the blast of the breath of his nostrils."

There are in these verses some very interesting points. Let's go over them together. First, where is God in this prophecy? He is in His temple. What happens when He hears? An earthquake, the stars quake, there is smoke and fire, thunder and lightning, and God's voice is heard. Then the channels of the sea appear and the foundations of the world are discovered. Note that this prophecy has all of the characteristics of these three events. There is a companion chapter to this one in Psalms 18. Let's look at a few verses of that chapter also.

Psalms 18:11, "He made darkness his secret place; his pavilion round about him *were* dark waters *and* thick clouds of the skies. 12 At the brightness *that was* before him his thick clouds passed, hail *stones* and coals of fire." Notice there are secrets of God here and coals of fire. The context of this scripture is David's plea to God for deliverance. This will be an important point to remember as we continue to study the meaning behind this prophecy. We will come back to this scripture but we need to read on to discover the meaning of these symbols. Another related prophecy is found in Haggai 2:5-9, "According to the word that I covenanted with you when ye came out of Egypt, so my spirit remaineth among you: fear ye not. 6 For thus saith the LORD of hosts; Yet once, it is a little while (in other words, not yet but later), and I will shake the heavens, and the earth, and the sea, and the dry land; 7 And I will shake all nations, and the desire of all nations shall come: and I will fill this house with glory, saith the LORD of hosts. 8 The silver is mine, and the gold is mine, saith the LORD of hosts. 9 The glory of this latter house shall be greater than of the former, saith the LORD of hosts: and in this place will I give peace, saith the LORD of hosts." More detail is added in this prophecy.

Note that the context of verse 5 is a promise of the Holy Spirit remaining among God's people. God says at some point in time He would shake the heavens, the earth, the sea, and the dry land as a special sign having to do with the Holy Spirit. Then there is the filling of His house with glory. And the glory of the latter house was greater than the former. The latter rain is to be more glorious than the former. Now is the time of the latter rain. These events are a special symbol that this is the time God will pour out the latter rain on the earth.

Notice what the following texts have to say about the latter rain. Hosea 6:3, "Then shall we know, *if* we follow on to know the LORD: his going forth is prepared as the morning; and he shall come unto us as the rain, as the latter *and* former rain unto the earth."

Joel 2:23, "Be glad then, ye children of Zion, and rejoice in the LORD your God: for he hath given you the former rain moderately, and he will cause to come down for you the rain, the former rain, and the latter rain in the first *month*."

Zechariah 10:1, "Ask ye of the LORD rain in the time of the latter rain; *so* the LORD shall make bright clouds, and give them showers of rain, to every one grass in the field."

James 5:7, "Be patient therefore, brethren, unto the coming of the Lord. Behold, the husbandman waiteth for the precious fruit of the earth, and hath long patience for it, until he receive the early and latter rain."

SHAKING HEAVEN & EARTH

Haggai was encouraging the Israelites to rebuild the temple. Was the glory of the rebuilt temple ever literally greater than Solomon's temple? No. This has to be symbolic because it was never literally fulfilled. Something else is meant here. First, Christ walked in that temple, much greater glory. Second, God is saying that the glory of the latter rain will be greater than the former, early rain. He is also saying that all of these signs are a special symbol of the time of the latter rain and the second coming of Jesus Christ.

Look at Jesus' words in Matthew 24:29-31 which says, "Immediately after the tribulation of those days shall the sun be darkened, and the moon shall not give her light, and the stars shall fall from heaven, and the powers of the heavens shall be shaken: And then shall appear the sign of the Son of man in heaven: and then shall all the tribes of the earth mourn, and they shall see the Son of man coming in the clouds of heaven with power and great glory. And he shall send his angels with a great sound of a trumpet, and they shall gather together his elect from the four winds, from one end of heaven to the other."

The next event listed in this prophecy after the powers of heaven are shaken is the second coming of Jesus Christ. Don't miss that significance. Jesus is about to come back again just as the angels promised the disciples He would in the following scripture. Acts 1:9, "And when he had spoken these things, while they beheld, he was taken up; and a cloud received him out of their sight. 10 And while they looked steadfastly toward heaven as he went up, behold, two men stood by them in white apparel; 11 Which also said, Ye men of Galilee, why stand ye gazing up into heaven? this same Jesus, which is taken up from you into heaven, shall so come in like manner as ye have seen him go into heaven." Jesus is about to descend from heaven in the clouds with all the angels with Him. Are you ready for that event?

The next obvious question to ask is when will that be? Are we really close to the second coming? Jesus answers that question for us in Matthew 24:34, "Verily I say unto you, This generation shall not pass, till all these things be fulfilled." I'm sure the disciples thought Jesus was talking about their generation but obviously that was not the case. The logical answer to what generation Jesus was talking about is that when you see the last of these signs fulfilled before Jesus' second coming, that generation won't pass away until He returns. The last sign in verse 31 is "the powers of the heavens shall be shaken." If you are reading this, are not elderly and you do not die an untimely death, you will see Jesus come in your lifetime. Isn't that an awesome thought? Now you know where we are in time.

There is another part of the prophecy in Haggai that tells us more about what will happen in world events after the shaking of heaven and earth. It is found in Haggai 2:21-23 and reads as follows, "Speak to Zerubbabel, governor of Judah, saying, I will shake the heavens and the earth; And I will overthrow the throne of kingdoms, and I will destroy the strength of the kingdoms of the heathen; and I will overthrow the chariots, and those that ride in them; and the horses and their riders shall come down, every one by the sword of his brother. In that day, saith the LORD of hosts, will I take thee, O Zerubbabel, my servant, the son of Shealtiel, saith the LORD, and will make thee as a signet: for I have chosen thee, saith the LORD of hosts."

God says that after the shaking of heaven and earth He will begin overthrowing nations and the strength of their armies. It appears also that transportation is going to be a problem as well (horses and their riders). This may be happening by the time this book is published. If not, it will be happening soon. Keep your eyes open and watch for it. He will do this for the purpose of using His people in a very special way. This prophecy says He will make them as a signet. A signet is a signature ring or a seal. God is saying He is about to place His seal on His people and reveal His glory. This is a very important point that we will come back to in the chapters on the Seal and Glory. For now, file it in your memory banks and we will explore it further in future chapters. God has a special purpose and plan for His people in these last days.

CHAPTER 5
PREVIOUS PROPHECY

You may be aware of some very significant events that fulfilled portions of the prophecy in Matthew 24 already. Another prophecy that goes with this one in Matthew is found in Revelation 6:12, 13, "And I beheld when he had opened the sixth seal, and, lo, there was a great earthquake; and the sun became black as sackcloth of hair, and the moon became as blood; and the stars of heaven fell unto the earth, even as a fig tree casteth her untimely figs, when she is shaken of a mighty wind."

This great earthquake was called the Lisbon Earthquake and also had a tsunami. It occurred in

1755 and to that time was the most terrible earthquake ever recorded. It extended from Greenland to America, over most of Europe, and Africa. A great part of Algiers was destroyed along with wiping out a town of eight to ten thousand near Morocco. The tsunami hit the coast of Spain, Portugal, and Africa. A wave 60 feet high hit Cadiz. A conservative estimate of the loss of life on that day is 90,000 people.

There was another event in our not so distant past called the Great Dark Day. It occurred on May 19, 1780. On this day there was an unaccountable darkening of the sun in the middle of the day all across the New England states in America. To the west it covered Connecticut, to the south all along the coast, and to the north as far as the American colonies extended. Candles had to be used, the chickens went to roost, cattle gathered in their pasture, schools were dismissed and the children fled for home. The most intense darkness was from just after 11 am until about an hour before sunset. The sun then appeared briefly, though obscured by a black heavy mist. The blackness after dark was extremely dark even though there was almost a full moon which rose at about 9pm. After midnight the darkness disappeared and the moon appeared like blood. Joel 2:31 tells us that, "The sun shall be turned into darkness, and the moon into blood, before the great and the terrible day of the LORD come." These things are in our history.

Another event in our history is the day the stars fell, November 13, 1833. The entire sky over the

United States for hours was filled with falling stars of a meteor shower. It was said that never did rain fall thicker in all directions. This continued from 2am until broad daylight. Revelation 6:13 says, "and the stars of heaven fell unto the earth, even as a fig tree casteth her untimely figs, when she is shaken of a mighty wind."

Now the last of these prophetic events have occurred. The powers of the heavens have been shaken on December 26, 2004. The last events of earth's history are about to occur. Do you know what they are? Do you know what is coming? God has revealed it and the time is now.

CHAPTER 6
LAST DAY PROPHECY

Let's look at another scripture that has many of these same events. Revelation 8:3-5, "And another angel came and stood at the altar, having a golden censer; and there was given unto him much incense, that he should offer it with the prayers of all saints upon the golden altar which was before the throne. And the smoke of the incense, *which came* with the prayers of the saints, ascended up before God out of the angel's hand. And the angel took the censer, and filled it with fire of the altar, and cast *it* into the earth: and there were voices, and thunderings, and lightnings, and an earthquake."

Note that there is fire and smoke and an earthquake in this text. This text begins in the temple in heaven at the altar of incense. Remember that in 2 Samuel 22 God heard from His temple as David was praying for deliverance and there was smoke, fire, and an earthquake also. Here in Revelation 8 the angel takes fire from off the altar of incense to fill the censer and casts it into the earth, not down. If the censer was cast down, it would signify the close of probation for Jesus would no longer be interceding for us as our High Priest in heaven. But the censer is cast into the earth which means something far different. We must discover what the fire and its being cast into the earth means. So there is fire and smoke, voices, thunderings and lightnings, and an earthquake and trumpets. Revelation 4:5 tells us that lightnings and thunderings and voices proceed from the throne of God. Revelation 1:10 tells us that Jesus voice sounds like a trumpet. There are more pieces of the puzzle that have been added with this text. Where else do we see these same events in scripture?

Exodus 19:16-19, "And it came to pass on the third day in the morning, that there were thunders and lightnings, and a thick cloud upon the mount, and the voice of the trumpet exceeding loud; so that all the people that *was* in the camp trembled. [17]And Moses brought forth the people out of the camp to meet with God; and they stood at the nether part of the mount. [18]And mount Sinai was altogether on a smoke, because the LORD descended upon it in fire:

and the smoke thereof ascended as the smoke of a furnace, and the whole mount quaked greatly. [19]And when the voice of the trumpet sounded long, and waxed louder and louder, Moses spake, and God answered him by a voice."

In this event God came down in fire, there was smoke, voices, thunders and lightnings, and an earthquake and trumpets. These are all of the same events as Revelation 8. Notice that what followed in Exodus 20 was the Ten Commandments.

1. "And God spake all these words, saying, I *am* the LORD thy God, which have brought thee out of the land of Egypt, out of the house of bondage. Thou shalt have no other gods before me.

2. Thou shalt not make unto thee any graven image, or any likeness *of any thing* that *is* in heaven above, or that *is* in the earth beneath, or that *is* in the water under the earth: Thou shalt not bow down thyself to them, nor serve them: for I the LORD thy God *am* a jealous God, visiting the iniquity of the fathers upon the children unto the third and fourth *generation* of them that hate me; And showing mercy unto thousands of them that love me, and keep my commandments.

3. Thou shalt not take the name of the LORD thy God in vain; for the LORD will not hold him guiltless that taketh his name in vain.

4. Remember the Sabbath day, to keep it holy. Six days shalt thou labour, and do all thy work: But the seventh day is the Sabbath of the LORD thy God: in it thou shalt not do any work, thou, nor thy son, nor thy daughter, thy manservant, nor thy maidservant, nor thy cattle, nor thy stranger that is within thy gates: For in six days the LORD made heaven and earth, the sea, and all that in them is, and rested the seventh day: wherefore the LORD blessed the Sabbath day, and hallowed it.

5. Honour thy father and thy mother: that thy days may be long upon the land which the LORD thy God giveth thee.

6. Thou shalt not kill.

7. Thou shalt not commit adultery.

8. Thou shalt not steal.

9. Thou shalt not bear false witness against thy neighbour.

10. Thou shalt not covet thy neighbour's house, thou shalt not covet thy neighbour's wife, nor his manservant, nor his maidservant, nor his ox, nor his ass, nor any thing that is thy neighbour's."

SHAKING HEAVEN & EARTH

And concluding with verse 18, "And all the people saw the thunderings, and the lightnings, and the noise of the trumpet, and the mountain smoking: and when the people saw it, they removed, and stood afar off."

All of the same elements are here in Exodus 19 and 20 in the giving of the Ten Commandments at Mount Sinai. What is God trying to tell us? The giving of the law is related to judgment. The Ten Commandments, or God's law that Jesus wrote with His finger in stone, is the law by which we are judged. I will show in the next chapter that it was in fact Jesus, before His incarnation, who wrote the Ten Commandments with His finger and gave them to Moses. Please note that this is not Moses' law but God's law. They are two very distinctly different laws. You need to understand the differences in these laws to understand this prophecy clearly. Let's explore these two laws together in this next chapter.

CHAPTER 7
THE TWO LAWS

The two laws in the Bible are the Law of God and the Law of Moses. The Law of God is called the Ten Commandments. The Law of Moses is called the Book of the law or Book of the covenant and the handwriting of ordinances. The ceremonial law is another term used to describe Moses' law. Both laws have commandments. The Old and New Testament writers often referred to both of these laws as just "the law," leaving the reader to discern which law is being referred to keeping in mind the context of the verse. This has led to some confusion and lumping of all law together. This should not be done as these two laws are different and for different purposes. Another cause of confusion is that inside of the Law of Moses, the Ten Commandments are repeated and expanded upon. Because of this, it is important that you understand the differences and purposes of these two laws.

The following are some of the scriptures that identify some of those differences. I will for ease of reading identify the texts referring to the Law of God with a "G," and the Law of Moses with an "M." I ask the reader to look at the scripture around the text given to discern the context if it is not obvious from the text itself. This writing is not meant to be exhaustive and include all of the texts on the subject (which might include most of the Bible), but representative of the main points of difference.

Here are a couple of examples of Moses' law in the New Testament.

M 1Corinthians 9:9, "For it is written in the law of Moses, Thou shalt not muzzle the mouth of the ox that treadeth out the corn. Doth God take care for oxen?"

M Luke 2:22, "And when the days of her purification according to the law of Moses were accomplished, they brought him to Jerusalem, to present *him* to the Lord."

You can see from these examples that there are different types of laws in Moses' law. Some are ceremonial, some civil, some health, and some are expanding on God's law.

Both laws were written but in different ways.

God (Jesus) wrote His law with His finger.

G Exodus 31:18, "And he gave unto Moses, when he had made an end of communing with him upon mount Sinai, two tables of testimony, tables of stone, written with the finger of God."

G Exodus 32:16, "And the tables *were* the work of God, and the writing *was* the writing of God, graven upon the tables."

God wrote His law with His finger in stone. I put Jesus in parentheses because of what Jesus said in John 8:58. "Jesus said unto them, Verily, verily, I say unto you, Before Abraham was, I am." When God was talking to Moses at the burning bush He said the following. Exodus 3:14, "And God said unto Moses, I AM THAT I AM: and he said, Thus shalt thou say unto the children of Israel, I AM hath sent me unto you." Jesus was claiming to be the God that spoke with Moses. That is why the Pharisees took up stones to stone Him in verse 59 of John chapter 8.

Moses wrote the law of Moses.

M Deuteronomy 31:24, "And it came to pass, when Moses had made an end of writing the words of this law in a book, until they were finished."

God's law was also spoken by God.

G Deuteronomy 5:22, "These words the LORD spoke unto all your assembly in the mount out of the midst of the fire, of the cloud, and of the thick darkness, with a great voice: and he added no more. And he wrote them in two tables of stone, and delivered them unto me."

The placement of these two laws was different also.

G Exodus 40:20, "And he took and put the testimony into the ark, and set the staves on the ark, and put the mercy seat above upon the ark."

It was very important that the mercy seat be above the law because without mercy (we call it grace) there is no forgiveness. It is also interesting and of significance that this seat is also called the judgment seat and is in fact the symbolic representation of the judgment seat of Christ which is in the sanctuary in heaven. Isn't it beautiful that the mercy seat and the judgment seat are the same seat? The gospel is in that fact. Mercy and judgment not only met at the cross but they also meet here in the sanctuary at the judgment seat of Christ which is the mercy seat.

Moses' law was not placed in the ark but beside it.

M Deuteronomy 31:26, "Take this book of the law, and put it in the side of the ark of the covenant of the LORD your God, that it may be there for a witness against thee."

Moses law was placed beside the ark, not in it. This symbolized its temporary nature and the fact that no one was to be judged by Moses' law. It was not under the judgment seat. It was also against us, or contrary to us as we shall see in a later text.

God's law identifies what sin is.

G Romans 7:7, "What shall we say then? *Is* the law sin? God forbid. Nay, I had not known sin, but by the law: for I had not known lust, except the law had said, Thou shalt not covet."

G Romans 3:20, "Therefore by the deeds of the law there shall no flesh be justified in his sight: for by the law *is* the knowledge of sin."

G 1John 3:4, "Whosoever committeth sin transgresseth also the law: for sin is the transgression of the law."

Moses law was added because of sin.

M Galatians 3:19, "Wherefore then *serveth* the law? It was added because of transgressions, till the seed should come to whom the promise was made; *and it was* ordained by angels in the hand of a mediator."

God's law is not grievous.

G 1John 5:3, "For this is the love of God, that we keep his commandments: and his commandments are not grievous."

Moses' law is contrary to us.

M Colossians 2:14, "Blotting out the handwriting of ordinances that was against us, which was contrary to us, and took it out of the way, nailing it to his cross."

God's law is Royal.

G James 2:8, "If ye fulfill the royal law according to the Scripture, Thou shalt love thy neighbor as thyself, ye do well."

Moses' law is an ordinance.

M Ephesians 2:15, "Having abolished in his flesh the enmity, *even* the law of commandments *contained* in ordinances; for to make in himself of twain one new man, *so* making peace."

God's law judges all and is the law of liberty.

G James 2:10, "For whosoever shall keep the whole law, and yet offend in one *point,* he is guilty of all. 11 For he that said, Do not commit adultery, said also, Do not kill. Now if thou commit no adultery, yet if thou kill, thou art become a transgressor of the law. 12 So speak ye, and so do, as they that shall be judged by the law of liberty."

Moses' law judges no man.

M Colossians 2:14, "Blotting out the handwriting of ordinances that was against us, which was contrary to us, and took it out of the way, nailing it to his cross; 15 *And* having spoiled principalities and powers, he made a show of them openly, triumphing over them in it. 16 Let no man therefore judge you in meat, or in drink, or in respect of a holy day, or of the new moon, or of the sabbath *days."*

Note that these sabbath days were the special sabbath days related to the feasts that were outlined in Moses' law, not the 7th day Sabbath of creation and God's law.

God's law is spiritual.

G Romans 7:14, "For we know that the law is spiritual: but I am carnal, sold under sin."

Moses' law is carnal.

M Hebrews 7:16, "Who is made, not after the law of a carnal commandment, but after the power of an endless life."

God's law is blessing and peace.

SHAKING HEAVEN & EARTH

G Proverbs 29:18, "Where *there is* no vision, the people perish: but he that keepeth the law, happy *is* he."

G Psalm 119:165, "Great peace have they which love thy law: and nothing shall offend them."

Moses' law has curses for disobedience.

M Deuteronomy 29:20, "The LORD will not spare him, but then the anger of the LORD and his jealousy shall smoke against that man, and all the curses that are written in this book shall lie upon him, and the LORD shall blot out his name from under heaven. 21 And the LORD shall separate him unto evil out of all the tribes of Israel, according to all the curses of the covenant that are written in this book of the law."

M Galatians 3:10, "For as many as are of the works of the law are under the curse: for it is written, Cursed *is* every one that continueth not in all things which are written in the book of the law to do them."

God's law is perfect and converts.

G Psalms 19:7, "The law of the LORD *is* perfect, converting the soul: the testimony of the LORD *is* sure, making wise the simple."

Moses' law made nothing perfect.

M Hebrews 7:19, "For the law made nothing perfect, but the bringing in of a better hope *did;* by the which we draw nigh unto God."

God's law is eternal.

G Matthew 5:17, "Think not that I am come to destroy the law, or the prophets: I am not come to destroy, but to fulfill. 18 For verily I say unto you, Till heaven and earth pass, one jot or one tittle shall in no wise pass from the law, till all be fulfilled. 19 Whosoever therefore shall break one of these least commandments, and shall teach men so, he shall be called the least in the kingdom of heaven: but whosoever shall do and teach *them,* the same shall be called great in the kingdom of heaven." (Note that these were Jesus' words.)

Moses' law was temporary.

M Colossians 2:14, "Blotting out the handwriting of ordinances that was against us, which was contrary to us, and took it out of the way, nailing it to his cross."

M Heb 8:13, "In that he saith, A new *covenant,* he hath made the first old. Now that which decayeth and waxeth old *is* ready to vanish away."

Moses' law was symbolic.

M Hebrews 9:9, "Which *was* a figure for the time then present, in which were offered both gifts and sacrifices, that could not make him that did the service perfect, as pertaining to the conscience; 10 *Which stood* only in meats and drinks, and divers washings, and carnal ordinances, imposed *on them* until the time of reformation."

God's law is the guide of life.

G Ecclesiastes 12:13, "Let us hear the conclusion of the whole matter: Fear God, and keep his commandments: for this *is* the whole *duty* of man. 14 For God shall bring every work into judgment, with every secret thing, whether *it be* good, or whether *it be* evil."

God's grace is that gift of forgiveness, peace, and power that enables us to grow up into Christ and keep His law.

G Acts 20:32, "And now, brethren, I commend you to God, and to the word of his grace, which is able to build you up, and to give you an inheritance among all them which are sanctified."

G Revelation 14:12, "Here is the patience of the saints: here *are* they that keep the commandments of God, and the faith of Jesus."

From these scriptures you can see the significant differences between God's and Moses' law. It is important to remember that God's law is eternal and an expression of His love and character. Moses' law in contrast was temporary, contrary to us, and pointed forward to Christ. God has promised to write His law on our hearts in the new covenant that Jesus ratified with His blood. Consider that if God could have changed His law, Jesus would not have had to die. Another interesting point is that in order to have grace, God's law must be in effect. If God's law did not exist or was not in effect, there would be nothing to have grace from, or be forgiven for, because sin is transgression of God's law. 1 John 3:4, "Whosoever committeth sin transgresseth also the law: for sin is the transgression of the law."

CHAPTER 8
THE SANCTUARY

Remembering that God is revealing His secrets in prophecy, listen as you read the words of this scripture. Psalms 27:5, "For in the time of trouble he shall hide me in his pavilion: in the secret of his tabernacle shall he hide me; he shall set me up upon a rock." There are many secrets in God's tabernacle. The entire sanctuary and its service was a form of prophecy. Other words we use for the tabernacle are temple or sanctuary. I want to give you an outline of the symbolic meanings of the sanctuary. This will provide a framework for placing the secrets of God that are being revealed.

LYLE K. NORTON

You will notice that some of the things in the sanctuary have multiple meanings and some have only one that we are aware of. All of them teach us something about God and salvation.

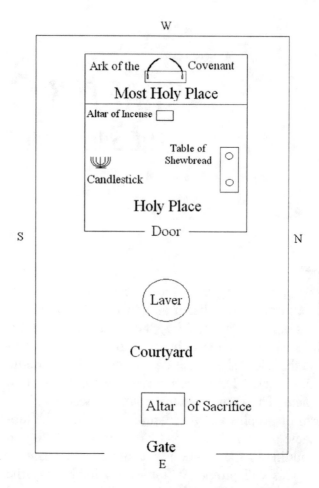

SHAKING HEAVEN & EARTH

Psalm 77:13, "Thy way, O God, *is* in the sanctuary: who *is so* great a God as *our* God?"

What does it mean that God's way is in the sanctuary? Remember what Jesus said in John 14:6? "Jesus saith unto him, I am the way the truth, and the life: no man cometh unto the Father, but by me."

Jesus' way is in the sanctuary. Is Jesus' way still in the sanctuary?

Psalms 27:5, "For in the time of trouble he shall hide me in his pavilion: in the secret of his tabernacle shall he hide me; he shall set me up upon a rock." Jesus is that Rock. Remember that the time of trouble is ahead of us, not in the past.

For what purpose did God say that He wanted to have the Israelites build the temple? Exodus 25:8, "And let them make me a sanctuary; that I may dwell among them. 9 According to all that I show thee, *after* the pattern of the tabernacle, and the pattern of all the instruments thereof, even so shall ye make *it*."

What pattern was shown to Moses? Hebrews 8:4, "For if he were on earth, he should not be a priest, seeing that there are priests that offer gifts according to the law: Who serve unto the example and shadow of heavenly things, as Moses was admonished of God when he was about to make the tabernacle: for, See, saith he, *that* thou make all things according to the pattern showed to thee in the mount. But Christ being come a high priest of good things to come, by a greater and more perfect tabernacle, not made with hands, that is to say, not of this building; 9:24, For Christ is not entered into the holy places made with hands, *which are* the figures of the true; but into heaven itself, now to appear in the presence of God for us."

The pattern shown to Moses was the pattern of the temple in heaven that Jesus is now in. Let's examine the meaning of the sanctuary in more detail to understand more about Jesus, His work, and the plan of salvation.

Gate/ Way/ Door

Exodus 27:16, "And for the gate of the court *shall be* a hanging of twenty cubits, *of* blue, and purple, and scarlet, and fine twined linen, wrought with needlework: *and* their pillars *shall be* four, and their sockets four."

There was only One gate, or way, into court.

John 14:6, "Jesus saith unto him, I am the way, the truth, and the life: no man cometh unto the Father, but by me." Jesus is the gate.

There was only One door into sanctuary.

John 10:9, "I am the door: by me if any man enter in, he shall be saved, and shall go in and out, and find pasture."

Jesus is the only gate, the only way, and the only door into heaven.

SHAKING HEAVEN & EARTH

The Courtyard

Revelation 11:1, "And there was given me a reed like unto a rod: and the angel stood, saying, Rise, and measure the temple of God, and the altar, and them that worship therein. But the court which is without the temple leave out, and measure it not; for it is given unto the Gentiles."

Why is the court left out? Because judgment begins at the house of God and those in the court (the world) have not entered into the house of God as yet.

1Peter 4:17, "For the time *is come* that judgment must begin at the house of God: and if *it* first *begin* at us, what shall the end *be* of them that obey not the gospel of God?"

We often think of judgment as beginning with the world but that is not scriptural. John in Revelation, Peter, and Ezekiel in Ezekiel 9 show us that God judges His church and His people first. This is also clear from the sanctuary service itself.

Altar of Sacrifice

Exodus 27:1, "And thou shalt make an altar *of* shittim wood, five cubits long, and five cubits broad; the altar shall be foursquare: and the height thereof *shall be* three cubits. And thou shalt make the horns of it upon the four corners thereof: his horns shall be of the same: and thou shalt overlay it with brass."

Hebrews 10:12, "But this man, after he had offered one sacrifice for sins forever, sat down on the right hand of God."

Where did Jesus offer His sacrifice? He was crucified on a cross. This means that the altar of sacrifice represents the cross.

Do we have a cross to bear also? Romans 12:1, "I beseech you therefore, brethren, by the mercies of God, that ye present your bodies a living sacrifice, holy, acceptable unto God, *which is* your reasonable service."

Romans 6:6, "Knowing this, that our old man is crucified with *him*, that the body of sin might be destroyed, that henceforth we should not serve sin."

We must come to the altar and surrender ourselves so that self can die and Christ can live in us. Galatians 2:20, "I am crucified with Christ: nevertheless I live; yet not I, but Christ liveth in me: and the life which I now live in the flesh I live by the faith of the Son of God, who loved me, and gave himself for me."

The Lamb

Leviticus 1:4, "And he shall put his hand upon the head of the burnt offering; and it shall be accepted for him to make atonement for him."

Exodus 12:5, "Your lamb shall be without blemish, a male of the first year: ye shall take *it* out from the sheep, or from the goats."

1Peter 1:19, "But with the precious blood of

Christ, as of a lamb without blemish and without spot."

Leviticus 5:5, "And it shall be, when he shall be guilty in one of these *things*, that he shall confess that he hath sinned in that *thing*: 6 And he shall bring his trespass offering unto the LORD for his sin which he hath sinned, a female from the flock, a lamb or a kid of the goats, for a sin offering; and the priest shall make an atonement for him concerning his sin."

John 1:29, "The next day John seeth Jesus coming unto him, and saith, Behold the Lamb of God, which taketh away the sin of the world."

It is clear from these texts that the lamb represents Jesus who gave His life for us, spotless and without blemish for He never sinned.

The Blood

Exodus 24:6, "And Moses took half of the blood, and put *it* in basins; and half of the blood he sprinkled on the altar. 7 And he took the book of the covenant, and read in the audience of the people: and they said, All that the LORD hath said will we do, and be obedient. 8 And Moses took the blood, and sprinkled *it* on the people, and said, Behold the blood of the covenant, which the LORD hath made with you concerning all these words."

Matthew 26:28, "For this is my blood of the new testament, which is shed for many for the remission of sins."

John 19:34, "But one of the soldiers with a spear pierced his side, and forthwith came there out blood and water."

Hebrews 9:18, "Whereupon neither the first *testament* was dedicated without blood. 19 For when Moses had spoken every precept to all the people according to the law, he took the blood of calves and of goats, with water, and scarlet wool, and hyssop, and sprinkled both the book, and all the people, 20 Saying, This *is* the blood of the testament which God hath enjoined unto you. 21 Moreover he sprinkled with blood both the tabernacle, and all the vessels of the ministry. 22 And almost all things are by the law purged with blood; and without shedding of blood is no remission. 23 *It was* therefore necessary that the patterns of things in the heavens should be purified with these; but the heavenly things themselves with better sacrifices than these. 24 For Christ is not entered into the holy places made with hands, *which are* the figures of the true; but into heaven itself, now to appear in the presence of God for us."

The literal things were at the ratification of the new covenant as the symbolic things were at the ratification of the old covenant. At the old there were blood and water, scarlet wool, and hyssop. At the new there was Jesus blood and water that flowed from His side. Scarlet represented the sin that Jesus bore on the cross. Wool represented the Lamb of God who was Jesus. Hyssop was used to hold up the sponge with gall of vinegar that Jesus was offered when He was thirsty. He tasted that bitterness so you and I could have living water that cleanses us, springing up into everlasting life.

The Laver

Exodus 30:17, "And the LORD spoke unto Moses, saying, 18 Thou shalt also make a laver *of* brass, and his foot *also of* brass, to wash *withal*: and thou shalt put it between the tabernacle of the congregation and the altar, and thou shalt put water therein. 19 For Aaron and his sons shall wash their hands and their feet thereat: 20 When they go into the tabernacle of the congregation, they shall wash with water, that they die not; or when they come near to the altar to minister, to burn offering made by fire unto the LORD: 21 So they shall wash their hands and their feet, that they die not."

Exodus 38:8, "And he made the laver *of* brass, and the foot of it *of* brass, of the looking glasses of *the women* assembling, which assembled *at* the door of the tabernacle of the congregation."

Isn't it interesting that the laver that was used to cleanse the priests was made from the mirrors of the women of Israel? We also have a choice symbolically to look in our mirrors and continue in vanity, or be cleansed.

John 3:5, "Jesus answered, Verily, verily, I say unto thee, Except a man be born of water and *of* the Spirit, he cannot enter into the kingdom of God."

Acts 2:38, "Then Peter said unto them, Repent,

and be baptized every one of you in the name of Jesus Christ for the remission of sins, and ye shall receive the gift of the Holy Ghost."

The laver represents baptism, repentance, and sanctification. The water washed the blood from the priest's hands as well as the dirt.

1John 5:6, "This is he that came by water and blood, *even* Jesus Christ; not by water only, but by water and blood. And it is the Spirit that beareth witness, because the Spirit is truth."

It is necessary to have both the blood and the water in our experience. We must have the forgiveness of God for sin and be justified and that requires the blood of the Lamb. We also must be cleansed from sin and that requires the washing of regeneration by the water and the Spirit. This is sanctification. We cannot have one without the other. Some have said that we need only the blood and not the water. This means that I only need to be forgiven and never need my life changed by God, just go on sinning. This is the doctrine and deeds of the Nicolaitanes which Jesus said He hated in Revelation 2:6, 15. Some have said they just need to live a good life (just the water) and God would accept them without them accepting Jesus and His blood. That too is not true. John 14:6, "Jesus saith unto him, I am the way, the truth, and the life: no man cometh unto the Father, but by me." We must have both the blood and the water.

SHAKING HEAVEN & EARTH

The Holy Place

This is the place where we receive spiritual light, food for our spirit, and offer our prayers before God's throne. It is God's presence or closeness which makes it holy. It is only God's special presence or blessing that makes anything holy. This represents the church. The articles of furniture in the Holy Place help us to understand how we are to live our lives as believers and are as follows.

Candlestick / Menorah

Exodus 25:31, "And thou shalt make a candlestick *of* pure gold: *of* beaten work shall the candlestick be made: his shaft, and his branches, his bowls, his knops, and his flowers, shall be of the same. 32 And six branches shall come out of the sides of it; three branches of the candlestick out of the one side, and three branches of the candlestick out of the other side: 33 Three bowls made like unto almonds, *with* a knop and a flower in one branch; and three bowls made like almonds in the other branch, *with* a knop and a flower: so in the six branches that come out of the candlestick. 34 And in the candlestick *shall be* four bowls made like unto almonds, *with* their knops and their flowers. 35 And *there shall be* a knop under two branches of the same, and a knop under two branches of the same, and a knop under two branches of the same, according to the six branches that proceed out of the candlestick. 36 Their knops and their branches shall be of the same: all it *shall be* one beaten work *of* pure gold. 37 And thou shalt make the seven lamps thereof: and they shall light the lamps thereof, that they may give light over against it. 38 And the tongs thereof, and the censers thereof, *shall be of* pure gold. 39 *Of* a talent of pure gold shall he make it, with all these vessels. 40 And look that thou make *them* after their pattern, which was showed thee in the mount."

Light

Exodus 27:20, "And thou shalt command the children of Israel, that they bring thee pure oil olive beaten for the light, to cause the lamp to burn always."

John 8:12, "Then spake Jesus again unto them, saying, I am the light of the world: he that followeth me shall not walk in darkness, but shall have the light of life."

Matthew 5:14, "Ye are the light of the world."

Philippians 2:15, "That ye may be blameless and harmless, the sons of God, without rebuke, in the midst of a crooked and perverse nation, among whom ye shine as lights in the world."

Lamp

John 15:5, "I am the vine, ye *are* the branches: He that abideth in me, and I in him, the same bringeth forth much fruit." Did you notice there is one central candlestick and six branches coming out of it? This represents the relationship we must have with Jesus. Without being attached to Him we get no oil and we cannot be a light.

Psalms 119:105, "Thy word *is* a lamp unto my feet, and a light unto my path." If we are not following God's word we are in darkness.

Revelation 4:5, "And out of the throne proceeded lightnings and thunderings and voices: and *there were* seven lamps of fire burning before the throne, which are the seven Spirits of God."

Oil

Exodus 25:6, "Oil for the light, spices for anointing oil, and for sweet incense."

Exodus 29:7, "Then shalt thou take the anointing oil, and pour *it* upon his head, and anoint him."

Matthew 25:3, "They that *were* foolish took their lamps, and took no oil with them: But the wise took oil in their vessels with their lamps."

James 5:14, "Is any sick among you? let him call for the elders of the church; and let them pray over him, anointing him with oil in the name of the Lord: And the prayer of faith shall save the sick, and the Lord shall raise him up; and if he have committed sins, they shall be forgiven him."

Oil represents the Holy Spirit which guides us into all truth, or light. Without the Holy Spirit we cannot understand truth or share it with anyone else. The Holy Spirit provides the power to understand

and obey God, just as the oil provides the fuel to make light.

Table of Showbread

Exodus 25:23-30, "Thou shalt also make a table *of* shittim wood: two cubits *shall be* the length thereof, and a cubit the breadth thereof, and a cubit and a half the height thereof. And thou shalt overlay it with pure gold, and make thereto a crown of gold round about. And thou shalt make unto it a border of a handbreadth round about, and thou shalt make a golden crown to the border thereof round about. And thou shalt make for it four rings of gold, and put the rings in the four corners that *are* on the four feet thereof. Over against the border shall the rings be for places of the staves to bear the table. And thou shalt make the staves *of* shittim wood, and overlay them with gold, that the table may be borne with them. And thou shalt make the dishes thereof, and spoons thereof, and covers thereof, and bowls thereof, to cover withal: *of* pure gold shalt thou make them. And thou shalt set upon the table shewbread before me always."

Leviticus 24:5-9, "And thou shalt take fine flour, and bake twelve cakes thereof: two tenth deals shall be in one cake. And thou shalt set them in two rows, six on a row, upon the pure table before the LORD. And thou shalt put pure frankincense upon *each* row, that it may be on the bread for a memorial, *even* an offering made by fire unto the LORD. Every Sabbath he shall set it in order before the LORD continually, *being taken* from the children of Israel by an everlasting covenant. And it shall be Aaron's and his sons'; and they shall eat it in the holy place: for it *is* most holy unto him of the offerings of the LORD made by fire by a perpetual statute."

John 6:31-35, "Our fathers did eat manna in the desert; as it is written, He gave them bread from heaven to eat. Then Jesus said unto them, Verily, verily, I say unto you, Moses gave you not that bread from heaven; but my Father giveth you the true bread from heaven. For the bread of God is he which cometh down from heaven, and giveth life unto the world. Then said they unto him, Lord, evermore give us this bread. And Jesus said unto them, I am the bread of life: he that cometh to me shall never hunger; and he that believeth on me shall never thirst."

Matthew 16:11, 12, "How is it that ye do not understand that I spake *it* not to you concerning bread, that ye should beware of the leaven of the Pharisees and of the Sadducees? Then understood they how that he bade *them* not beware of the leaven of bread, but of the doctrine of the Pharisees and of the Sadducees."

Unleavened bread represents the true doctrine of Christ while leavened bread represents the tainted doctrines of all others.

Altar of Incense

Exodus 30:1, "And thou shalt make an altar to burn incense upon: *of* shittim wood shalt thou make it."

Exodus 30:6-9, "And thou shalt put it before the veil that *is* by the ark of the testimony, before the mercy seat that *is* over the testimony, where I will meet with thee. And Aaron shall burn thereon sweet incense every morning: when he dresseth the lamps, he shall burn incense upon it. And when Aaron lighteth the lamps at even, he shall burn incense upon it, a perpetual incense before the LORD throughout your generations. Ye shall offer no strange incense thereon, nor burnt sacrifice, nor meat offering; neither shall ye pour drink offering thereon."

Luke 1:10, "And the whole multitude of the people were praying without at the time of incense."

Revelation 8:3, 4, "And another angel came and stood at the altar, having a golden censer; and there was given unto him much incense, that he should offer *it* with the prayers of all saints upon the golden altar which was before the throne. And the smoke of the incense, *which came* with the prayers of the saints, ascended up before God out of the angel's hand."

The incense represents the prayers of the saints and the intercession of Christ who offers up our prayers, with His, to the Father.

SHAKING HEAVEN & EARTH

The Veil

Exodus 26:33, "And thou shalt hang up the veil under the tacks, that thou mayest bring in thither within the veil the ark of the testimony: and the veil shall divide unto you between the holy *place* and the most holy."

Hebrews 6:19, 20, "Which *hope* we have as an anchor of the soul, both sure and steadfast, and which entereth into that within the veil; Whither the forerunner is for us entered, *even* Jesus, made a high priest forever after the order of Melchizedek."

Hebrews 9:3, "And after the second veil, the tabernacle which is called the holiest of all."

Hebrews 10:20, "By a new and living way, which he hath consecrated for us, through the veil, that is to say, his flesh."

A veil was placed on God's Son, a body of flesh, so that we could see His true character.

The Most Holy Place

The Most Holy Place represents the dwelling place and throne of God. It is called the most holy place because of God's special presence there. This is the apartment where the visible manifestation of God would appear as the Shekinah glory. There was only one article of furniture in this room.

Exodus 26:34, "And thou shalt put the mercy seat upon the ark of the testimony in the most holy *place.*"

Hebrews 9:24, 25, "For Christ is not entered into the holy places made with hands, *which are* the figures of the true; but into heaven itself, now to appear in the presence of God for us: Nor yet that he should offer himself often, as the high priest entereth into the most holy place every year with blood of others."

Ark of the Testimony/Covenant

Psalms 80:1, "Give ear, O Shepherd of Israel, thou that leadest Joseph like a flock; thou that dwellest *between* the cherubims, shine forth."

Psalms 99:1, "The LORD reigneth; let the people tremble: he sitteth *between* the cherubims; let the earth be moved."

Isaiah 37:16, "O LORD of hosts, God of Israel, that dwellest *between* the cherubims, thou *art* the God, *even* thou alone, of all the kingdoms of the earth: thou hast made heaven and earth."

The Mercy Seat

Exodus 25:17-22, "And thou shalt make a mercy seat *of* pure gold: two cubits and a half *shall be* the length thereof, and a cubit and a half the breadth thereof. And thou shalt make two cherubims *of* gold, *of* beaten work shalt thou make them, in the two ends of the mercy seat. And make one cherub on the one end, and the other cherub on the other end: *even* of the mercy seat shall ye make the cherubims on the two ends thereof. And the cherubims shall stretch forth *their* wings on high, covering the mercy seat with their wings, and their faces *shall look* one to another; toward the mercy seat shall the faces of the cherubims be. And thou shalt put the mercy seat above upon the ark; and in the ark thou shalt put the testimony that I shall give thee. And there I will meet with thee, and I will commune with thee from above the mercy seat, from between the two cherubims which *are* upon the ark of the testimony, of all *things* which I will give thee in commandment unto the children of Israel."

Psalms 85:7-11, "Show us thy mercy, O LORD, and grant us thy salvation. I will hear what God the LORD will speak: for he will speak peace unto his people, and to his saints: but let them not turn again to folly. Surely his salvation *is* nigh them that fear him; that glory may dwell in our land. Mercy and truth are met together; righteousness and peace have kissed *each other*. Truth shall spring out of the earth; and righteousness shall look down from heaven."

Romans 14:10, "But why dost thou judge thy brother? or why dost thou set at naught thy brother? for we shall all stand before the judgment seat of Christ."

2Corinthians 5:10, "For we must all appear before the judgment seat of Christ; that every one may receive the things *done* in *his* body, according to that he hath done, whether *it be* good or bad."

The mercy seat is also called the judgment seat. The law of God is under the mercy seat indicating that both judgment and mercy must meet the requirements of the law. The requirements are perfect obedience or death. The blood of the sacrifice on the

Day of Atonement was placed on the mercy seat to satisfy the requirement of the law. The reader should note that without the law there is nothing to have mercy from and there is no judgment. Judgment comes from interpreting the law. Mercy is available to the violator only by someone else paying the penalty that the law requires. You may have to read that twice to get it, but basically, without the law you don't need mercy or grace.

Hebrews 4:16, "Let us therefore come boldly unto the throne of grace, that we may obtain mercy, and find grace to help in time of need."

Hebrews 1:3, "Who being the brightness of *his* glory, and the express image of His person, and upholding all things by the word of his power, when he had by himself purged our sins, sat down on the right hand of the Majesty on high."

Revelation 14:6, 7, "And I saw another angel fly in the midst of heaven, having the everlasting gospel to preach unto them that dwell on the earth, and to every nation, and kindred, and tongue, and people, Saying with a loud voice, Fear God, and give glory to him; for the hour of his judgment is come: and worship him that made heaven, and earth, and the sea, and the fountains of waters."

Isaiah 1:27, "Zion shall be redeemed with judgment, and her converts with righteousness."

Aaron's Rod that Budded

Numbers 17:1-10, "And the LORD spoke unto

Moses, saying, Speak unto the children of Israel, and take of every one of them a rod according to the house of *their* fathers, of all their princes according to the house of their fathers twelve rods: write thou every man's name upon his rod. And thou shalt write Aaron's name upon the rod of Levi: for one rod *shall be* for the head of the house of their fathers. And thou shalt lay them up in the tabernacle of the congregation before the testimony, where I will meet with you. And it shall come to pass, *that* the man's rod, whom I shall choose, shall blossom: and I will make to cease from me the murmurings of the children of Israel, whereby they murmur against you. And Moses spoke unto the children of Israel, and every one of their princes gave him a rod apiece, for each prince one, according to their fathers' houses, *even* twelve rods: and the rod of Aaron *was* among their rods. And Moses laid up the rods before the LORD in the tabernacle of witness. And it came to pass, that on the morrow Moses went into the tabernacle of witness; and, behold, the rod of Aaron for the house of Levi was budded, and brought forth buds, and bloomed blossoms, and yielded almonds. And Moses brought out all the rods from before the LORD unto all the children of Israel: and they looked, and took every man his rod. And the LORD said unto Moses, Bring Aaron's rod again before the testimony, to be kept for a token against the rebels; and thou shalt quite take away their murmurings from me, that they die not."

The buds, blossoms, and almonds on Aaron's rod had the same emblems as the candlestick and represented that the priests were to be teachers of God's truth. In other words, just as the candlestick was an instrument through which the oil (the Holy Spirit) flowed to give light (the Bible and God's truths), the priests were also an instrument for the same purpose.

Deuteronomy 24:8, "Take heed in the plague of leprosy, that thou observe diligently, and do according to all that the priests the Levites shall teach you: as I commanded them, *so* ye shall observe to do."

Leprosy is a symbol of sin. The priests were to teach truth in order for the learner to be cleansed from leprosy. It is the truth that sets you free from sin.

Pot of Manna

Exodus 16:33, 34, "And Moses said unto Aaron, Take a pot, and put an omer full of manna therein, and lay it up before the LORD, to be kept for your generations. As the LORD commanded Moses, so Aaron laid it up before the Testimony, to be kept."

God miraculously provided food for the Israelites in the wilderness and preserved that food in the ark. This is a symbol and reminder that God provides for both our physical and spiritual needs.

SHAKING HEAVEN & EARTH

The Ten Commandments/God's Law

Exodus 25:16, "And thou shalt put into the ark the testimony which I shall give thee."

This was God's law that He wrote with His finger on two tables of stone and spoke from Mt. Sinai. It is the law that defines sin.

1John 3:4, "Whosoever committeth sin transgresseth also the law: for sin is the transgression of the law."

Moses' Law

Deuteronomy 31:24, "And it came to pass, when Moses had made an end of writing the words of this law in a book, until they were finished, 25 That Moses commanded the Levites, which bore the ark of the covenant of the LORD, saying, 26 Take this book of the law, and put it in the side of the ark of the covenant of the LORD your God, that it may be there for a witness against thee."

Colossians 2:14, "Blotting out the handwriting of ordinances that was against us, which was contrary to us, and took it out of the way, nailing it to his cross."

Moses' law was put on the side of the ark showing its temporary nature until the cross. Its placement also shows that we are not to be judged by Moses' law because it was not placed under the mercy seat (judgment seat).

Galatians 3:24, "Wherefore the law was our

schoolmaster *to bring us* unto Christ, that we might be justified by faith."

The law of Moses was a schoolmaster and the sanctuary service was a school to bring us to Christ. The purpose of the school was to teach about Jesus. Both the law of Moses and the earthly sanctuary service were nailed to the cross and ceased to function as an active exercise. That being said, the lessons they teach are not to be forgotten or neglected, because they teach us about salvation and about the ministry of Jesus on our behalf.

The High Priest

Leviticus 21:10-12, "And *he that is* the high priest among his brethren, upon whose head the anointing oil was poured, and that is consecrated to put on the garments, shall not uncover his head, nor rend his clothes; Neither shall he go in to any dead body, nor defile himself for his father, or for his mother; Neither shall he go out of the sanctuary, nor profane the sanctuary of his God; for the crown of the anointing oil of his God *is* upon him: I *am* the LORD."

Hebrews 3:1, "Wherefore, holy brethren, partakers of the heavenly calling, consider the Apostle and High Priest of our profession, Christ Jesus."

Hebrews 4:14, "Seeing then that we have a great high priest, that is passed into the heavens, Jesus the Son of God, let us hold fast *our* profession."

Hebrews 8:1-13, "Now of the things which we

have spoken *this is* the sum: We have such a high priest, who is set on the right hand of the throne of the Majesty in the heavens; A minister of the sanctuary, and of the true tabernacle, which the Lord pitched, and not man. For every high priest is ordained to offer gifts and sacrifices: wherefore *it is* of necessity that this man have somewhat also to offer. For if he were on earth, he should not be a priest, seeing that there are priests that offer gifts according to the law: Who serve unto the example and shadow of heavenly things, as Moses was admonished of God when he was about to make the tabernacle: for, See, saith he, *that* thou make all things according to the pattern showed to thee in the mount. But now hath he obtained a more excellent ministry, by how much also he is the mediator of a better covenant, which was established upon better promises. For if that first *covenant* had been faultless, then should no place have been sought for the second. For finding fault with them, he saith, Behold, the days come, saith the Lord, when I will make a new covenant with the house of Israel and with the house of Judah: Not according to the covenant that I made with their fathers in the day when I took them by the hand to lead them out of the land of Egypt; because they continued not in my covenant, and I regarded them not, saith the Lord. For this *is* the covenant that I will make with the house of Israel after those days, saith the Lord; I will put my laws into their mind, and write them in their hearts: and I will be to them a God, and they shall be to me a people: And they shall not teach every man his neighbor, and every man his brother, saying, Know the Lord: for all shall know me, from the least to the greatest. For I will be merciful to their unrighteousness, and their sins and their iniquities will I remember no more. In that he saith, A new *covenant,* he hath made the first old. Now that which decayeth and waxeth old *is* ready to vanish away."

I know these symbols are a lot to absorb all at once. You may have to go over them several times to understand the basics of each symbol. You may want to review them at a later time to refresh your memory. These symbols teach us important truths about Jesus and salvation. They are also very important keys that will help you understand the prophecies this book is written about. Let's continue with a very important event the sanctuary pointed forward to.

CHAPTER 9
THE DAY OF ATONEMENT

Look back at Revelation 8:3-5. The angel is standing at the altar of incense and much incense is given to him. This was only to happen on the Day of Atonement and only to be done by the High Priest. In the daily service only a pinch of incense was used by the common priests. On the Day of Atonement, much incense was used by the High Priest.

You may remember that in the daily service the sinner came and confessed his sin on the head of the lamb. The lamb was then slain and the blood of the lamb was taken by the priest into the sanctuary and sprinkled before the veil. These symbolic acts transferred the sin from the sinner to the lamb and through the blood of the lamb to the sanctuary where it was stored until the Day of Atonement.

Note the following from Leviticus 16:12, 13 regarding the Day of Atonement, "And he shall take a censer full of burning coals of fire from off the altar before the LORD, and his hands full of sweet incense beaten small, and bring it within the veil: 13 And he shall put the incense upon the fire before the LORD, that the cloud of the incense may cover the mercy seat that is upon the testimony, that he die not."

The Day of Atonement is synonymous with the Day of Judgment. It is the cleansing of the sanctuary of all the sins that are stored there. The people have either the seal of God given to them or they are pronounced Satan's and the judgment of death given.

After the cloud of incense smoke covered the mercy seat the high priest would sprinkle the blood on the mercy seat toward the east and then before the mercy seat 7 times. The sprinkling of blood eastward is symbolic of the sealing angel that comes from the east in Revelation 7:2, "And I saw another angel ascending from the east, having the seal of the living God." The sprinkling of the blood before the mercy seat 7 times has important significance also. We will come back to this point, but here is the bottom line.

Hebrews 8:1, "Now of the things which we have

spoken this is the sum: We have such an high priest, who is set on the right hand of the throne of the Majesty in the heavens; 2 A minister of the sanctuary, and of the true tabernacle, which the Lord pitched, and not man."

Christ is our High Priest. He is symbolized by the angel spoken of in Revelation 8:3-5. He is interceding for us in the heavenly sanctuary. Even more specifically, He is administering the intercession of the Day of Atonement right now. Ten days before the Day of Atonement trumpets were blown and the people were called to "sanctify themselves," or confess and repent of their sins, until the Day of Atonement. The trumpet would also blow on the Day of Atonement only in the year of Jubilee. Notice what happens in Revelation 8:6, "And the seven angels which had the seven trumpets prepared themselves to sound." The trumpet is about to blow.

On the Day of Atonement the high priest would cast lots on the 2 goats choosing one to represent Christ and the other (the scapegoat) to represent Satan. The goat representing Christ was sacrificed and the High Priest would take the blood to apply in the most holy place.

We need to discover what the fire from the altar represents as that is a very important aspect of this service on the Day of Atonement as well as the daily service. Let's look at a vision of Isaiah to discover the meaning.

Isaiah 6:1-7, "In the year that king Uzziah died I saw also the Lord sitting upon a throne, high and lifted up, and his train filled the temple. Above it stood the seraphims: each one had six wings with twain he covered his face, and with twain he covered his feet, and with twain he did fly. And one cried unto another, and said, Holy, holy, holy, *is* the LORD of hosts: the whole earth *is* full of his glory. And the posts of the door moved at the voice of him that cried, and the house was filled with smoke.

Then said I, Woe *is* me! for I am undone; because I *am* a man of unclean lips, and I dwell in the midst of a people of unclean lips: for mine eyes have seen the King, the LORD of hosts.

Then flew one of the seraphims unto me, having a live coal in his hand, *which* he had taken with the tongs from off the altar: And he laid *it* upon my mouth, and said, Lo, this hath touched thy lips; and thine iniquity is taken away, and thy sin purged."

The live coal, or fire from the altar, is for the purpose of purging and removing our sin. John 16:7, 8 tells us, "Nevertheless I tell you the truth; It is expedient for you that I go away: for if I go not away, the Comforter will not come unto you; but if I depart, I will send him unto you. And when he is come, he will reprove the world of sin, and of righteousness, and of judgment." It is the Holy Spirit that reproves us of sin and gives us power to obey. Notice this verse in John 1:12, "But as many as received him, to them gave he power to become the sons of God, *even* to them that believe on his name." The fire from the altar represents the Holy Spirit.

Remember what happened to Nadab and Abihu when they brought fire of their own kindling to the altar. God had commanded only to use fire that He had kindled. Leviticus 10:1, "And Nadab and Abihu, the sons of Aaron, took either of them his censer, and put fire therein, and put incense thereon, and offered strange fire before the LORD, which he commanded them not. 2 And there went out fire from the LORD, and devoured them, and they died before the LORD." Why was the strange fire so important? They were essentially saying that their works, or righteousness, were good enough. Only the righteousness of Christ that is given to us by the Holy Spirit is good enough. All our righteousness is filthy rags.

Let's look back to the Day of Atonement again. The high priest would take the censer filled with fire from the altar of incense that was kindled by God. The High Priest then would take finely ground incense representing the intercession, righteousness and merits of Christ, and as he stepped through the veil into the most holy place would put all of the incense on the live coals of the censer. A great smoke, which represents the prayers of the saints, would go up and cover the mercy seat, also representing Christ standing between those who have through prayer confessed their sins and the righteous judgment of the law under the mercy seat. The mercy seat is also the judgment seat of Christ. If you have received Christ through His representative, the Holy Spirit; the judgment of Christ is mercy. If you have not allowed the Holy Spirit to dwell in you and have grieved Him away; the judgment of Christ is death, which is the penalty for sin. This is the judgment that Nadab and Abihu received.

But what about the ringing sound of the bell. We read the following in Exodus 28:34, 35, "A golden bell and a pomegranate, a golden bell and a pomegranate, upon the hem of the robe round about. And it shall be upon Aaron to minister: and his sound shall be heard when he goeth in unto the holy *place* before the LORD, and when he cometh out, that he die not." The sound of the bell was only heard on the Day of Atonement when the High Priest went into the Most Holy place. The bell has rung in our galaxy with the sound of an F sharp. Jesus is ministering in the sanctuary in heaven on the Day of Atonement. Everything in the earthly sanctuary service represented something in the heavenly. Jesus is doing His last work as a High Priest. The cleansing of the sanctuary is almost over. He is about to remove His priestly robe and put on His kingly garments and our probationary time will be over.

The high priest applied the blood 7 times in the most holy and then came out indicating that the temple was cleansed of those sins, placed his hands on the scapegoat (representing Satan) thus transferring the sins of those whose sin is forgiven through the blood of Jesus to Satan the originator of sin.

Notice in vs. 6 of Revelation 8 that there are 7 messages that Christ, the one who speaks with the voice of a trumpet (Revelation 1:10), gives from the throne of God. These 7 trumpets contain spiritual messages for us that we need for this special time. There are elements of history and elements of prophecy in the 7 trumpets but there are also future messages of warning to the world. They are symbolized by the sprinkling of the blood 7 times before the mercy seat. They are 7 last opportunities to receive mercy from Christ. If we reject these messages of mercy we will receive the 7 last plagues. We need to study and understand these messages. They are soon to be given.

When the Day of Atonement in heaven is over, Jesus will no more be our High Priest interceding for us. There will be no more opportunity to be forgiven. There will be no more sins transferred to the sanctuary in heaven. All the sins of the forgiven will have been transferred to Satan and all the sins of the unforgiven must be born by those that committed them. We will come back to this point and discuss it further in the chapter on the sealing and probation. Just remember the important work that Jesus, our High Priest, is doing for us at this moment on the Day of Atonement.

CHAPTER 10
EARTHQUAKES

Earthquakes are of great significance both historically and prophetically in the Bible. They are markers of time periods and a sign of God's judgment as we shall learn in the following scriptures.

The first earthquake ever recorded is found in the history of Noah's flood. Genesis 7:11 says, "In the six hundredth year of Noah's life, in the second month, the seventeenth day of the month, the same day were all the fountains of the great deep broken up, and the windows of heaven were opened."

The fountains of the great deep breaking up had

to be the most catastrophic earthquake in history. This first earthquake is comparable to one of the last earthquakes foretold in the Bible as part of the seventh plague. Revelation 16:17, "And the seventh angel poured out his vial into the air; and there came a great voice out of the temple of heaven, from the throne, saying, It is done. 18 And there were voices, and thunders, and lightnings; and there was a great earthquake, such as was not since men were upon the earth, so mighty an earthquake, *and* so great. 19 And the great city was divided into three parts, and the cities of the nations fell: and great Babylon came in remembrance before God, to give unto her the cup of the wine of the fierceness of his wrath. 20 And every island fled away, and the mountains were not found. 21 And there fell upon men a great hail out of heaven, *every stone* about the weight of a talent: and men blasphemed God because of the plague of the hail; for the plague thereof was exceeding great."

The important thing we want to look at in the flood earthquake is that God used this first earthquake as judgment against the antediluvian people. Genesis 6:5 says, "And GOD saw that the wickedness of man *was* great in the earth, and *that* every imagination of the thoughts of his heart *was* only evil continually. 6 And it repented the LORD that he had made man on the earth, and it grieved him at his heart. 7 And the LORD said, I will destroy man whom I have created from the face of the earth; both man, and beast, and the creeping thing, and the fowls of the air; for it repenteth me that I have made them. 8 But Noah found grace in the eyes of the LORD."

This earthquake was a judgment of God and marked the end of an era and the beginning of another time. This is an important precedent that is established in scripture. It is also an important precedent that we find grace, as Noah did, before the last earthquakes in this earth's history.

The next earthquake recorded was at Mount Sinai. Exodus 19:18, "And mount Sinai was altogether on a smoke, because the LORD descended upon it in fire: and the smoke thereof ascended as the smoke of a furnace, and the whole mount quaked greatly."

At this earthquake the basis for all judgment was given. God's Holy law, the Ten Commandments, gives the law by which sin is defined and the rules by which we will be judged. This earthquake also ended one era and set up a new era, one in which the children of Israel were God's chosen people living under the old covenant.

The next literal earthquake mentioned was a symbolic example to Elijah on Mount Horeb (see I Kings 19) and a prophetic one to us. Shortly after this earthquake Elijah was translated to heaven. This earthquake was a type of the one that occurs at the seventh plague shortly before we are translated.

The next earthquake in the sequence is one during the reign of Uzziah king of Judah. Uzziah began his reign following God but then he became proud and lifted up in his own eyes. He worshiped in a way contrary to what God had outlined. He went into the temple and offered incense himself. The priests of God came in and resisted him, telling him he should not do that. Uzziah became angry and God smote him with leprosy. The apostasy of the leader of the people of God in worship was marked by a great earthquake. This earthquake was one of judgment on God's chosen people. Are you beginning to see a pattern?

This earthquake also was a type of another earthquake in our future. A leader of a church professing God will advocate worshiping God in a way not proscribed by God. Look at the prophecy of that earthquake. Revelation 11:13, "And the same hour was there a great earthquake, and the tenth part of the city fell, and in the earthquake were slain of men seven thousand: and the remnant were affrighted, and gave glory to the God of heaven. 14 The second woe is past; *and,* behold, the third woe cometh quickly."

The second woe refers to the sixth trumpet of Revelation 9, as the three woes are the fifth, sixth, and seventh trumpets. When you study the prophecies of Revelation you will understand that this occurs after a false form of worship is mandated by a leader of a country and a church just as Uzziah was. There has been confusion about the 7 trumpets because they have dual application much as the coming of Elijah prophecy in Malachi had dual application. Jesus spoke of that prophecy as applying to John the Baptist even though there is clearly another application to the time of the end. The 7 trumpets have prophetic application in a timeline from the time of Christ through to the second coming of Christ. They also have a spiritual message application and I believe a second prophetic application after the tsunami earthquake. The context and placement of the verses in Revelation 8:2, 6 indicate this. The spiritual messages of the 7 trumpets will be of special significance in the near future. This is a special aspect of what the events and prophecies of the tsunami earthquake point out. The 7 trumpets are about to sound and we should pay special attention to these messages that Jesus who speaks with the voice of a trumpet gives as they are the last messages of mercy from God.

There is another earthquake of which this earthquake during Uzziah's reign is a type. Look at the following prophecy regarding Jesus. Zechariah 14:4, "And his feet shall stand in that day upon the mount of Olives, which *is* before Jerusalem on the east, and the mount of Olives shall cleave in the midst thereof toward the east and toward the west, *and there shall be* a very great valley; and half of the mountain shall remove toward the north, and half of it toward the south. 5 And ye shall flee *to* the valley of the mountains; for the valley of the mountains shall reach unto Azal: yea, ye shall flee, like as ye fled from before the earthquake in the days of Uzziah king of Judah: and the LORD my God shall come, *and* all the saints with thee."

This is the place that Jesus makes ready for the New Jerusalem that comes down out of heaven in Revelation 21. As His feet touch the Mount of Olives there is a great earthquake, the mountain splits and makes a great plain, the resting place for the New Jerusalem.

The next two earthquakes are the most significant earthquakes in the Bible. Look at the following scriptures. Matthew 27:50, "Jesus, when he had cried again with a loud voice, yielded up the ghost. 51 And, behold, the veil of the temple was rent in twain from the top to the bottom; and the earth did quake, and the rocks rent; 52 And the graves were opened; and many bodies of the saints which slept arose, 53 And came out of the graves after his resurrection, and went into the holy city, and appeared unto many."

Matthew 28:1, "In the end of the Sabbath, as it began to dawn toward the first *day* of the week, came Mary Magdalene and the other Mary to see the sepulcher. 2 And, behold, there was a great earthquake: for the angel of the Lord descended from heaven, and came and rolled back the stone from the door, and sat upon it. 3 His countenance was like lightning, and his raiment white as snow."

These earthquakes at the death and resurrection of Jesus marked the end of the old covenant and the beginning of the new covenant. They also marked the ultimate judgment of God against sin in the sacrifice of His Son to pay the penalty for breaking God's Holy law.

SHAKING HEAVEN & EARTH

From this point on there is a difference in the earthquakes in the Bible. Remember that at the earthquake when Jesus died, the graves of saints were opened, and then at the earthquake of Jesus resurrection, these saints were raised from the dead with Jesus. From this point on there is not only judgment but deliverance for God's people in the earthquakes of the scriptures.

The first example after this time is of Paul and Silas deliverance from prison. Acts 16:23, "And when they had laid many stripes upon them, they cast *them* into prison, charging the jailer to keep them safely: 24 Who, having received such a charge, thrust them into the inner prison, and made their feet fast in the stocks. 25 And at midnight Paul and Silas prayed, and sang praises unto God: and the prisoners heard them. 26 And suddenly there was a great earthquake, so that the foundations of the prison were shaken: and immediately all the doors were opened, and every one's bands were loosed."

I want to point out that from this point on we have a unique problem in looking at earthquakes. The problem is identified in the following scripture. Matthew 24:7, "For nation shall rise against nation, and kingdom against kingdom: and there shall be famines, and pestilences, and earthquakes, in divers places." The point is that Jesus is prophesying that as we near the end of time that there are going to be a multitude of earthquakes. So the question is, how do we identify specific earthquakes to be ones that are prophesied? The answer is that all of the other specific earthquakes that are prophesied have other events or identifying marks that are associated with them. You will see that as we go through these last earthquakes.

The next earthquake in scripture is the one at the opening of the sixth seal. Revelation 6:12, "And I beheld when he had opened the sixth seal, and, lo, there was a great earthquake; and the sun became black as sackcloth of hair, and the moon became as blood; 13 And the stars of heaven fell unto the earth, even as a fig tree casteth her untimely figs, when she is shaken of a mighty wind."

You can see that in this prophecy there are other events that let us know which earthquake is the earthquake of this prophecy. The Great Dark Day occurred on May 19, 1780 and the moon was as blood that night. The stars fell on November 13, 1833. In the prophecy the sequence is clearly delineated. First there is a "great earthquake," the sun becomes black, the moon becomes as blood, and finally, the stars fall. The Lisbon earthquake in 1755 is the only earthquake that is "great," and precedes the sun being blackened, the moon appearing as blood, and the stars falling. Because of the sequence and the character of the specific events we can positively identify this earthquake as the specific earthquake of this prophecy.

The next earthquake is the one this book is written about. Revelation 8:5, "And the angel took the censer, and filled it with fire of the altar, and cast *it* into the earth: and there were voices, and thunderings, and lightnings, and an earthquake."

Joel 3:16, "The LORD also shall roar out of Zion, and utter his voice from Jerusalem; and the heavens and the earth shall shake: but the LORD *will be* the hope of his people, and the strength of the children of Israel."

Haggai 2 also states, "I will shake the heavens, and the earth, and the sea, and the dry land." 2 Samuel 22 tells us that "the channels of the sea appeared and the foundations of the world were discovered."

God wanted us to be sure that we were able to identify this earthquake so He connected it in prophecy with all these events and signs. When you list them out, it is a significant list that rules out chance due to the laws of probability. The earthquake is associated with the foundations of the heavens shaking, the channels of the sea, the dry land, and the foundations of the world, fire, and smoke. All of these elements occurred in association with this earthquake. It leaves no room for doubt that this is the earthquake prophesied.

The earthquake that follows the tsunami earthquake is one of special judgment by God. Many of the prophecies in the previous verses of Revelation chapter 11 have had fulfillment in the past. However, some particulars were not fulfilled and this earthquake is one of those particulars. This suggests to us that there are dual applications of these prophecies just as there is a dual application in other prophecies. Verse 14 says that this earthquake occurs at the end of the sixth trumpet because it says, "the second woe is past." As I mentioned, the first, second, and third woes are synonymous with the fifth, sixth, and seventh trumpets

Some have suggested that this earthquake prophecy is symbolic and refers to some other event besides a literal earthquake; however, we face some significant problems in arriving at that conclusion. First, all of the other references in Revelation to earthquakes are about literal earthquakes. In fact, all of the other references to earthquakes in the whole Bible are about literal earthquakes. Why would this one be different? Second, the conclusion was arrived at because it does not fit the theology for the 7 trumpets being only in our history. Revelation chapter 7 shows us that the fullness of the 7 trumpets does not occur until after the sealing of God's church. The beginning of chapter 8, with the placement of the tsunami earthquake prophecy between the 7 angels being given 7 trumpets and the 7 angels preparing themselves to sound, shows us very clearly that there is a future application to the 7 trumpets. This does not negate the fact that there were also applications to some of the particulars in these 7 trumpets in the past. God has the wisdom and ability to give us prophecies that have more than one meaning and more than one application.

Here is the earthquake in Revelation 11:13, "And the same hour was there a great earthquake, and the tenth part of the city fell, and in the earthquake were slain of men seven thousand: and the remnant were affrighted, and gave glory to the God of heaven. 14 The second woe is past; *and,* behold, the third woe cometh quickly." There are a number of specifics in this earthquake also. It is against a certain city and people of that city. Verse 8 identifies which city it will occur in as it is "where also our Lord was crucified." This means that this earthquake will occur in Jerusalem in our near future.

This prophecy is also connected, because of its location, sequence, and judgment aspect, with a prophecy in Daniel 11:45 which reads, "And he shall plant the tabernacles of his palace between the seas in the glorious holy mountain; yet he shall come to his end, and none shall help him." The glorious holy mountain refers to Jerusalem (see Daniel 9:16) and coming to his end may be because of this earthquake. This prophecy also tells us that another power or authority will move his palace, or place of rulership, to Jerusalem. Revelation 18 says that his end comes with violence and his city is burned. It appears that this earthquake is part of those events.

The next earthquake is one that occurs at the end of the 7th trumpet. Revelation 11:15, "And the seventh angel sounded; and there were great voices in heaven, saying, The kingdoms of this world are become *the kingdoms* of our Lord, and of his Christ; and he shall reign forever and ever. 16 And the four and twenty elders, which sat before God on their seats, fell upon their faces, and worshiped God, 17

Saying, We give thee thanks, O Lord God Almighty, which art, and wast, and art to come; because thou hast taken to thee thy great power, and hast reigned. 18 And the nations were angry, and thy wrath is come, and the time of the dead, that they should be judged, and that thou shouldest give reward unto thy servants the prophets, and to the saints, and them that fear thy name, small and great; and shouldest destroy them which destroy the earth. 19 And the temple of God was opened in heaven, and there was seen in his temple the ark of his testament: and there were lightnings, and voices, and thunderings, and an earthquake, and great hail."

We will be able to identify this earthquake by our "seeing" the ark and the law as well as the great hail that is associated with it. Whether the "seeing" is literal or figurative is a valid question. It may well be that this is a symbolic "seeing," meaning that somehow attention is brought to the law of God that everyone is aware of and cannot help but "see."

The next earthquake is also with hail but it is when the seventh plague is given. Revelation 16:17, "And the seventh angel poured out his vial into the air; and there came a great voice out of the temple of heaven, from the throne, saying, It is done. 18 And there were voices, and thunders, and lightnings; and there was a great earthquake, such as was not since men were upon the earth, so mighty an earthquake, *and* so great. 19 And the great city was divided into three parts, and the cities of the nations fell: and great Babylon came in remembrance before God, to give unto her the cup of the wine of the fierceness of his wrath. 20 And every island fled away, and the mountains were not found. 21 And there fell upon men a great hail out of heaven, *every stone* about the weight of a talent: and men blasphemed God because of the plague of the hail; for the plague thereof was exceeding great."

Isaiah gives another prophecy about this earthquake. As the events of this earthquake unfold it leads directly into the second coming of Jesus. This apparently is within a few days or hours of this event. Isaiah 2:19, "And they shall go into the holes of the rocks, and into the caves of the earth, for fear of the LORD, and for the glory of his majesty, when he ariseth to shake terribly the earth. 20 In that day a man shall cast his idols of silver, and his idols of gold, which they made *each one* for himself to worship, to the moles and to the bats; 21 To go into the clefts of the rocks, and into the tops of the ragged rocks, for fear of the LORD, and for the glory of his majesty, when he ariseth to shake terribly the earth."

Isaiah 13:9, "Behold, the day of the LORD cometh, cruel both with wrath and fierce anger, to lay the land desolate: and he shall destroy the sinners thereof out of it. 10 For the stars of heaven and the constellations thereof shall not give their light: the sun shall be darkened in his going forth, and the moon shall not cause her light to shine. 11 And I will punish the world for *their* evil, and the wicked for their iniquity; and I will cause the arrogance of the proud to cease, and will lay low the haughtiness of the terrible. 12 I will make a man more precious than fine gold; even a man than the golden wedge of Ophir. 13 Therefore I will shake the heavens, and the earth shall remove out of her place, in the wrath of the LORD of hosts, and in the day of his fierce anger."

The following is a summary list of these earthquakes in the sequence of occurrence and with the texts where they are found for easy reference.

1. Noah's flood earthquake – Judgment of God on the antediluvian world- End of the antediluvian era - Genesis 7:11
2. Earthquake at the giving of the Ten Commandments on Mt. Sinai – Basis of all Judgment - Marks the beginning of the old covenant era - Exodus 19:18
3. Elijah's earthquake on Mt. Horeb – Type of Seventh plague earthquake- 1 Kings 19:11
4. King Uzziah's earthquake – Type of earthquake that punishes Babylon power for false worship just as it punished Uzziah's kingdom for false worship - Zechariah 14:5, 2 Chronicles 26:16-21
5. Earthquake at Jesus Death – Judgment against sin - Graves of many saints opened - End of old covenant era and ratification of new covenant - Matthew 27:50-53
6. Earthquake at Jesus Resurrection – Judgment

and Deliverance of Righteous – Many saints resurrected with Jesus – Matthew 28:1-3
7. Paul and Silas delivered by earthquake- Acts 16:23-26
8. Lisbon earthquake in 1755 – Opening of 6th Seal – Deliverance of God's people from the persecuting power of the 1260 year prophecy – Beginning of the time of the end era - Revelation 6:12, 13
9. Tsunami Earthquake 2004 – Deliverance of God's people in giving Latter Rain Holy Spirit – Era of the Latter Rain and Day of Atonement Judgment - Revelation 8:5
10. Judgment earthquake on Babylon power that institutes false worship and deliverance of God's people from the beast power that is persecuting them – Centers in Jerusalem - Revelation 11:13
11. 7th Trumpet earthquake revealing God's Holy Law as the standard of Judgment and Righteousness – Deliverance of God's people who keep His commandments - Revelation 11:15-19
12. 7th Plague earthquake immediately preceding the 2nd Coming of Jesus- Signals that probationary time is over – Final deliverance of God's people - Revelation 16:17, Isaiah 2:19-21, 13:9-13, 29:6
13. Mount of Olives earthquake after the millennium when Jesus feet touch the earth preparing a place for the New Jerusalem coming down from heaven – Deliverance of the earth - Zechariah 14:4

You can see that the next event in prophecy after the Tsunami earthquake of 2004 is the institution of a false worship set up by the Babylon power. We know this from other prophecies as well but we can see that the next earthquake foretold is one that punishes this power for false worship. Therefore, we know that the beast power will require worship of his image and himself next in the sequence.

Now you have a picture of all the earthquakes in the Bible. There are more secrets of God hidden in these prophecies and events for you to search out and discover. Keep studying as you will be blessed by it.

CHAPTER 11
VISION OF DRY BONES

Ezekiel was given an unusual vision about dry bones. There are numerous things that we can draw and learn from this vision; however, the tsunami earthquake prophecies give special light to this vision that can help us understand more of what God is trying to tell us. First, here is the vision.

Ezekiel 37:1, "The hand of the LORD was upon me, and carried me out in the spirit of the LORD, and set me down in the midst of the valley which *was* full of bones, 2 And caused me to pass by them round about: and, behold, *there were* very many in the open valley; and, lo, *they were* very dry.

3 And he said unto me, Son of man, can these bones live? And I answered, O Lord GOD, thou knowest.

4 Again he said unto me, Prophesy upon these bones, and say unto them, O ye dry bones, hear the word of the LORD. 5 Thus saith the Lord GOD unto these bones; Behold, I will cause breath to enter into you, and ye shall live: 6 And I will lay sinews upon you, and will bring up flesh upon you, and cover you with skin, and put breath in you, and ye shall live; and ye shall know that I *am* the LORD.

7 So I prophesied as I was commanded: and as I prophesied, there was a noise, and behold a shaking, and the bones came together, bone to his bone. 8 And when I beheld, lo, the sinews and the flesh came up upon them, and the skin covered them above: but *there was* no breath in them.

9 Then said he unto me, Prophesy unto the wind, prophesy, son of man, and say to the wind, Thus saith the Lord GOD; Come from the four winds, O breath, and breathe upon these slain, that they may live.

10 So I prophesied as he commanded me, and the breath came into them, and they lived, and stood up upon their feet, an exceeding great army.

11 Then he said unto me, Son of man, these bones are the whole house of Israel: behold, they say, Our bones are dried, and our hope is lost: we are cut off for our parts. 12 Therefore prophesy and

say unto them, Thus saith the Lord GOD; Behold, O my people, I will open your graves, and cause you to come up out of your graves, and bring you into the land of Israel. 13 And ye shall know that I *am* the LORD, when I have opened your graves, O my people, and brought you up out of your graves, 14 And shall put my spirit in you, and ye shall live, and I shall place you in your own land: then shall ye know that I the LORD have spoken *it*, and performed *it*, saith the LORD."

This vision is about the church of God in the last days. God says that the vision is about the "whole house of Israel." Galatians 3:29 says, "And if ye *be* Christ's, then are ye Abraham's seed, and heirs according to the promise." The Christian church today is the "whole house of Israel."

The people of God are as dry bones. We in the church may not like to see ourselves that way; however, compared to what God desires us to be that is what we are like. What brings the people of God together, gives them a proper body, and finally puts breath in them? The answer is prophecy.

In verses 1 and 2 God shows Ezekiel these bones and Ezekiel notes that these bones are very dry. Then, in verse 3, God asks him if these bones can live. Notice his answer. "O Lord GOD, thou knowest." In other words, Ezekiel doesn't see any way these dry bones can live and the situation to his eye is hopeless. He does however, affirm his faith that with God nothing shall be impossible.

Ezekiel is told to prophesy three times in this

vision. In the first prophecy it appears that everything is provided for the people to live, and indeed, they are promised that they will live. In verse 7 Ezekiel prophesies, and in addition to the body parts coming together and being formed, there are two significant things that happen. There is a noise and a shaking. When you look at these two words in the original language, Strong's Concordance states the word for noise can also be translated "thunder or voice" and the word for shaking can also be translated "earthquake." These are the same words found in Revelation 8:5, "And the angel took the censer, and filled it with fire of the altar, and cast *it* into the earth: and there were voices, and thunderings, and lightnings, and an earthquake."

The vision of the dry bones is talking about the experience of God's people as they receive and understand these prophecies and the power of the Holy Spirit that is promised in these prophecies. The fact that when Ezekiel gave the first prophecy there were voices, thunder, and an earthquake, tells us what prophecies were received. It also tells us the time in which the prophecy is set. The time is now at the end of time. These are messages and power from God that will revive God's people, even from dry bones.

After Ezekiel pronounces the first prophecy bringing the dry bones together, forming sinews, flesh, and skin, the bodies are still not alive. Why are they not alive? God said that they will live. We know that God does nothing wrong and He has provided everything they need. The only reasonable conclusion is that something in them (the people of the dry bones) is missing and has to take place first. But God does not leave them in this lifeless state. He provides more prophecy. Why is prophecy so important? The answer is found in Revelation 19:10 the last part which reads, "the testimony of Jesus is the spirit of prophecy."

Without understanding prophecy you cannot truly understand who Jesus is and what His character is like. In short, you cannot have the testimony of Jesus without the spirit of prophecy. Doesn't that make prophecy more important?

In verse 9 God tells Ezekiel to prophesy to the wind that breath will come from the four winds. We need to understand what these four winds are so let's look at another scripture. This scripture is a vision that was given to Zechariah in Zechariah 6:1, "And I turned, and lifted up mine eyes, and looked, and, behold, there came four chariots out from between two mountains; and the mountains *were* mountains of brass. 2 In the first chariot *were* red horses; and in the second chariot black horses; 3 And in the third chariot white horses; and in the fourth chariot grizzled and bay horses.

4 Then I answered and said unto the angel that talked with me, What *are* these, my lord? 5 And the angel answered and said unto me, These *are* the four spirits of the heavens, which go forth from standing before the Lord of all the earth."

The word translated spirits in verse 5 is the

same word that is translated wind and breath, as well as spirit, in Ezekiel. This gives us a context to understand the meaning of the four winds. They are the four spirits that stand before God. These spirits have a specific task or function that is given them by God. Let's continue in Zechariah's vision.

6 "The black horses which *are* therein go forth into the north country; and the white go forth after them; and the grizzled go forth toward the south country. 7 And the bay went forth, and sought to go that they might walk to and fro through the earth: and he said, Get you hence, walk to and fro through the earth. So they walked to and fro through the earth. 8 Then cried he upon me, and spoke unto me, saying, Behold, these that go toward the north country have quieted my spirit in the north country."

The expression that they "walk to and fro" which results in the Lord's spirit being quieted is important in this vision. In Job 1:7 when Satan is asked by God what he is doing at a princes meeting in heaven, Satan replies that he has come, "From going to and fro in the earth, and from walking up and down in it." The implication is that the inhabitants of the earth have chosen him and he is the ruler or "rightful prince" of the earth. That is when God asks if he has considered His servant Job.

From this understanding we can see what the four winds, or four spirits of God walking to and fro, are doing. They are causing people to come to a decision for God or for Satan. That is what creates peace or "quiets" God's spirit. There is no longer war within the individual regarding their choice. They have chosen who they are going to serve.

The second prophecy of Ezekiel in this vision of the dry bones is one that causes the people to make a decision for or against God. That is the function of the four winds. That is what the prophecies and messages of the 7 trumpets will do. There is another aspect to this that will further clarify this function. In verse 11 the people of God give the reason why they were dry bones. "Our bones are dried, and our hope is lost." They have no hope. In other words, they are discouraged and discouragement paralyzes faith. You cannot have absolute trust in God and have no hope. Absolute trust in God gives you hope. This is another aspect of what the four winds, or spirits, give to the people of God. They renew their hope. This is another aspect of what prophecy gives to those that receive it. It gives hope.

There is then one more prophecy God tells Ezekiel to give in this vision. God says to prophesy that He will bring them out of their graves, put His spirit in them, and put them in their own land. Soon God will resurrect His saints by the power of His Spirit and take them to the Promised Land.

We need a new life. We need to be born again and grow up into mature Christians. In order for that to happen we need God's Holy Spirit. Without God's Spirit it is impossible, just as impossible as dry bones coming to life.

There's a land that God has promised to His people. Hebrews 11:8, "By faith Abraham, when he was called to go out into a place which he should after receive for an inheritance, obeyed; and he went out, not knowing whither he went. 9 By faith he sojourned in the land of promise, as *in* a strange country, dwelling in tabernacles with Isaac and Jacob, the heirs with him of the same promise: 10 For he looked for a city which hath foundations, whose builder and maker *is* God."

Ezekiel doesn't tell us what happens when he fulfills the Lord's command to prophesy the third time, but we know it will be glorious. Glory is the reason for these prophecies. Glory is our reason for living.

CHAPTER 12
GLORY

In Revelation 8:5 we see the ministering of our High Priest, we see judgment taking place, and there is more. Let's look at another prophecy that ties this all together. Hebrews 12:18-29, "For ye are not come unto the mount that might be touched, and that burned with fire, nor unto blackness, and darkness, and tempest, 19And the sound of a trumpet, and the voice of words; which voice they that heard entreated that the word should not be spoken to them any more: 20(For they could not endure that which was commanded, And if so much as a beast touch the mountain, it shall be stoned, or thrust through with a dart: 21And so terrible was the sight, that Moses said, I exceedingly fear and quake:) 22But ye are come unto mount Sion, and unto the city of the living God, the heavenly Jerusalem, and to an innumerable company of angels, 23To the general assembly and church of the firstborn, which are written in heaven, and to God the Judge of all, and to the spirits of just men made perfect, 24And to Jesus the mediator of the new covenant, and to the blood of sprinkling, that speaketh better things than that of Abel.

25See that ye refuse not him that speaketh. For if they escaped not who refused him that spake on earth, much more shall not we escape, if we turn away from him that speaketh from heaven: 26Whose voice then shook the earth: but now he hath promised, saying, Yet once more I shake not the earth only, but also heaven. 27And this word, Yet once more, signifieth the removing of those things that are shaken, as of things that are made, that those things which cannot be shaken may remain. 28Wherefore we receiving a kingdom which cannot be moved, let us have grace, whereby we may serve God acceptably with reverence and godly fear: 29For our God is a consuming fire."

At Sinai God's voice shook the earth and the people entered into the old covenant saying, "All that You have said we will do." Here God is shaking the heavens and the earth, reaffirming His new covenant promise of the Holy Spirit and writing His law on our hearts. It also is a symbol of the last time the Holy Spirit is to be poured out, the latter rain. Why? So that the Holy Spirit can finish the work in the world and in us, because our God, who is a consuming fire to sin, is about to come back.

What happens after the powers of heaven are shaken? Jesus comes back. What is the glory that Haggai was talking about? What was shaken? Heaven and earth were shaken. What is it that cannot be moved? What is it that God has told us we are to take with us to heaven? Christ's character the Holy Spirit is building in us. What is it that Haggai was giving encouragement for building? The temple of God that had been destroyed was what needed to be rebuilt. 1 Corinthians 3:16, "Know ye not that ye are the temple of God, and that the Spirit of God dwelleth in you?" Ephesians 2:21, 22, "In whom all the building fitly framed together groweth unto an holy temple in the Lord: 22In whom ye also are builded together for an habitation of God through the Spirit."

We as Christians have not fully understood what Paul has written. We like parts of his writing but reject other parts because we think that is impossible. The clearest dissertation that Paul gives about glory is found in 2 Corinthians chapter 3. I feel this is so important that I am putting the entire chapter here for you to read. I pray that God will give you grace to understand this revelation of glory.

2 Corinthians 3:1, "Do we begin again to commend ourselves? or need we, as some *others,* epistles of commendation to you, or *letters* of

commendation from you?

2 Ye are our epistle written in our hearts, known and read of all men: 3 F*orasmuch as ye are* manifestly declared to be the epistle of Christ ministered by us, written not with ink, but with the Spirit of the living God; not in tables of stone, but in fleshy tables of the heart. 4 And such trust have we through Christ to God-ward: 5 Not that we are sufficient of ourselves to think any thing as of ourselves; but our sufficiency *is* of God; 6 Who also hath made us able ministers of the new testament; not of the letter, but of the spirit: for the letter killeth, but the spirit giveth life.

7 But if the ministration of death, written *and* engraven in stones, was glorious, so that the children of Israel could not steadfastly behold the face of Moses for the glory of his countenance; which *glory* was to be done away: 8 How shall not the ministration of the spirit be rather glorious? 9 For if the ministration of condemnation *be* glory, much more doth the ministration of righteousness exceed in glory. 10 For even that which was made glorious had no glory in this respect, by reason of the glory that excelleth. 11 For if that which is done away *was* glorious, much more that which remaineth *is* glorious.

12 Seeing then that we have such hope, we use great plainness of speech: 13 And not as Moses, *which* put a veil over his face, that the children of Israel could not steadfastly look to the end of that which is abolished: 14 But their minds were

blinded: for until this day remaineth the same veil untaken away in the reading of the old testament; which *veil* is done away in Christ. 15 But even unto this day, when Moses is read, the veil is upon their heart.

16 Nevertheless when it shall turn to the Lord, the veil shall be taken away. 17 Now the Lord is that Spirit: and where the Spirit of the Lord *is,* there *is* liberty. 18 But we all, with open face beholding as in a glass the glory of the Lord, are changed into the same image from glory to glory, *even* as by the Spirit of the Lord."

This is the glory of God in the promise of the new covenant. He has promised to write His Holy Law of liberty, not in stone as He did at Sinai, but in our hearts. Jesus died to save us from our sins. The law of liberty, truth and love that the Holy Spirit writes on our hearts sets us free from sin and death. This is the glory that is to lighten the whole earth in Revelation 18:1, "And after these things I saw another angel come down from heaven, having great power; and the earth was lightened with his glory." The promise of God to do these things is also to give us hope. Hope strengthens and saves us, Romans 8:24.

Hebrews 12 and Haggai 2 are telling us that Christ shakes the heaven and the earth to give the glory of His character to His people. Christ in you the hope of glory, Colossians 1:27. 2 Samuel 22 and Revelation 8:3-5 tell us that Jesus is ministering in the heavenly sanctuary on the Day of

Atonement, the time of judgment. "Fear God, and give glory to him; for the hour of his judgment is come: and worship him that made heaven, and earth, and the sea, and the fountains of waters," Revelation 14:7. This is the reason for these tremendous events. To awaken the sleeping saints and warn them to get ready, allow God to place His glory, Christ's character in you. Matthew 24 tells us that we are at the end of the time of the end and Jesus is about to return to take His people to the Promised Land.

CHAPTER 13
THE SEALING & PROBATION

Revelation 7:1 tells us, "And after these things I saw four angels standing on the four corners of the earth, holding the four winds of the earth, that the wind should not blow on the earth, nor on the sea, nor on any tree." These 4 angels are holding the 4 winds that they won't blow on the earth, the sea, or trees. John is seeing the elements of nature—earthquake, hurricane and tornado, and political strife—represented as being held by four angels. These winds are under control until God gives the word to let them go. In other words, in order for the tsunami earthquake to have happened, these 4 angels are starting to let go.

It is important however, not to miss Revelation 7:3, "Hurt not the earth, neither the sea, nor the trees, till we have sealed the servants of our God in their foreheads." The first trumpet (Rev. 8:7) hurts the earth and the trees. The second (Rev. 8:8) hurts the sea. In the 5th trumpet (Rev. 9:4) it says to hurt only those who don't have the seal of God in their foreheads. This is saying that the fullness of the trumpets is not given until God's people are sealed. What this means is that the sealing of God's church and people happen between Revelation 8:6 and Revelation 8:7, in other words, now. Even though there has been a prophetic application to much of the 7 trumpets that has already occurred, the spiritual messages contained in these trumpets have not been given. There is also further prophetic application of the 7 trumpets that has not yet happened. One of the significant reasons for the prophecies foretelling the tsunami earthquake and the related events is to bring our attention to the 7 trumpets and that they are about to sound. We have not understood the importance of these messages that Christ, the one who speaks with the voice of a trumpet, gives. We have not understood partly because we thought they were mostly in the past and partly because, until recently, they were not present truth. Now they are present truth. We need to prayerfully study these messages.

What is the sealing? What does it mean and how does it happen? Let's explore this together. 2 Timothy 2:19 says, "Nevertheless the foundation of God standeth sure, having this seal, The Lord knoweth them that are his. And, Let every one that nameth the name of Christ depart from iniquity." This tells us that the seal is placed by God on those that He knows are His. Further, it is placed on those who have departed from iniquity. That is another way of saying those who have stopped sinning. How is this done?

Ephesians 4:30, "And grieve not the Holy Spirit of God, whereby ye are sealed unto the day of redemption." The power to overcome sin is given by the Holy Spirit. John 1:12, "But as many as received him, to them gave he power to become the sons of God, *even* to them that believe on his name: 13 Which were born, not of blood, nor of the will of the flesh, nor of the will of man, but of God."

It is only by faith in Jesus Christ and acceptance of His Holy Spirit that our hearts can be changed and our lives become like His. We cannot do this work by willpower by our own effort. It is only God dwelling in us that can overcome sin and make us like Jesus. Paul, here in Ephesians, is warning us not to grieve, or resist and push away, the Holy Spirit. The seal is the likeness of Christ that is placed in us by the Holy Spirit.

There is another text that makes this point even clearer. 1John 3:1-9, "Behold, what manner of love the Father hath bestowed upon us, that we should be called the sons of God: therefore the world knoweth us not, because it knew him not. 2 Beloved, now are we the sons of God, and it doth not yet appear what we shall be: but we know that, when he shall appear, we shall be like him; for we shall see him as he is. 3 And every man that hath this hope in him purifieth himself, even as he is pure. 4 Whosoever committeth sin transgresseth also the law: for sin is the transgression of the law. 5 And ye know that he was manifested to take away our sins; and in him is no sin. 6 Whosoever abideth in him sinneth not: whosoever sinneth hath not seen him, neither known him. 7 Little children, let no man deceive you: he that doeth righteousness is righteous, even as he is righteous. 8 He that committeth sin is of the devil; for the devil sinneth from the beginning. For this purpose the Son of God was manifested, that he might destroy the works of the devil. 9 Whosoever is born of God doth not commit sin; for his seed remaineth in him: and he cannot sin, because he is born of God." God and sin cannot dwell in the same place. Our work is to allow God to dwell in us. That is how we "purify" ourselves and allow Christ to "destroy the works of the devil."

In Revelation 8:6 we are told that the 7 angels who have the 7 trumpets are preparing themselves to sound. We see from Revelation 7:3 that they are not to sound until the servants of God are sealed. The sealing time for God's church is about to close. If your miss everything else, don't miss this point! When the sealing is over, probation is closed for God's people!

1 Peter 4:17, "For the time *is come* that judgment must begin at the house of God." Ezekiel 9

SHAKING HEAVEN & EARTH

also makes it clear that God's people are judged first. Then there is a short time remaining that the spiritual messages of the 7 trumpets are given to the world before their probationary time also closes.

Some have said that we don't need to consider these things because God won't do anything to His people. Consider the following text. Zephaniah 1:12, "And it shall come to pass at that time, *that* I will search Jerusalem with candles, and punish the men that are settled on their lees: that say in their heart, The LORD will not do good, neither will he do evil." Jerusalem represents God's church and His people. Are you prepared to be searched with the light of God?

This is explained another way in the following text. Revelation 14:14-20, "And I looked, and behold a white cloud, and upon the cloud *one* sat like unto the Son of man, having on his head a golden crown, and in his hand a sharp sickle. 15 And another angel came out of the temple, crying with a loud voice to him that sat on the cloud, Thrust in thy sickle, and reap: for the time is come for thee to reap; for the harvest of the earth is ripe. 16 And he that sat on the cloud thrust in his sickle on the earth; and the earth was reaped.

17 And another angel came out of the temple which is in heaven, he also having a sharp sickle. 18 And another angel came out from the altar, which had power over fire; and cried with a loud cry to him that had the sharp sickle, saying, Thrust in thy sharp sickle, and gather the clusters of the vine of the

earth; for her grapes are fully ripe. 19 And the angel thrust in his sickle into the earth, and gathered the vine of the earth, and cast *it* into the great winepress of the wrath of God. 20 And the winepress was trodden without the city, and blood came out of the winepress, even unto the horse bridles, by the space of a thousand *and* six hundred furlongs."

From this text we see that there are two distinct reapings of the harvest of the world. Jesus performs the first reaping and an angel performs the second reaping. The first is for God's church and the second is for the rest of the world. Probation for God's church closes first. We in the church may not like this truth; however, it is truth nonetheless. Time is truly running out.

Jesus tells this story another way in Matthew 25. There are 10 maids of honor who are awaiting the groom. All of them have lamps but only 5 have gotten more oil before the time of the wedding. They all fall asleep because of the delay in the groom's arrival. At midnight the call is heard, "He's coming!" All trim their lamps when the call is heard. All 10 of these maids of honor represent those in the church. All have the Bible (the lamps) and all have the Holy Spirit (the oil) and all have seen truth (the light). All fall asleep because of the delay (have you been sleeping?). The only difference is that 5 have additional oil in their vessels which represents the special outpouring of the Holy Spirit in the latter rain. It is almost midnight. The time to get this oil is now, at any cost.

CHAPTER 14
THE ELIJAH MESSAGE

Elijah had a message for the people. "How long halt ye between two opinions? If the Lord be God, follow Him: but if Baal, then follow him." I Kings 18:21. Baal was the sun god and was worshiped on the venerable day of the sun, or Sunday. God was worshiped on the Sabbath, the 7th day of creation that He had blessed and made holy. We now call it Saturday. Take special note of God's words that He spoke and wrote with His finger in the 4th commandment found in Exodus 20:8, "Remember the Sabbath day, to keep it holy. Six days shalt thou labour, and do all thy work: But the seventh day is the Sabbath of the LORD thy God: in it thou shalt not do any work, thou, nor thy son, nor thy daughter, thy manservant, nor thy maidservant, nor thy cattle, nor thy stranger that is within thy gates: For in six days the LORD made heaven and earth, the sea, and all that in them is, and rested the seventh day: wherefore the LORD blessed the Sabbath day, and hallowed it." This commandment is the only one that identifies God as the creator, tells what He has created, and specifies a time that is set apart for holy use. These are all the elements of a seal, the authority of an individual, the area of that authority, and a date or time of authority. Are you willing to allow God to write His law in your heart and place His seal on you?

Look at the words of Elijah's prayer, 1 Kings 18:37, "Hear me, O LORD, hear me, that this people may know that thou *art* the LORD God, and *that* thou hast turned their heart back again. 38 Then the fire of the LORD fell, and consumed the burnt sacrifice, and the wood, and the stones, and the dust, and licked up the water that *was* in the trench."

When Elijah prayed, fire came down from heaven that the people would know that God had turned their heart back again. What changes our hearts? It is only the Holy Spirit that can change our hearts. This is the same message that is found in Haggai chapter 2. Are you willing to allow God to change your heart and give you glory?

Then Elijah prayed for rain and sent his servant 7 times to look for rain. On the 7th time the servant saw a cloud about the size of a man's hand. Elijah's message is to be given now. God has sent His fire, He has done everything He can to turn our hearts to Him. He has told us to pray for the latter rain of the Holy Spirit. There are 7 messages of warning in the 7 trumpets and 7 plagues if we don't receive those messages. At the end of the 7th trumpet the mystery of God is finished and we see the sign of the Son of man as Elijah's servant did. Only this time, the cloud grows brighter and larger and larger until we see Jesus.

Christ is standing at the altar of incense, ministering in the heavenly sanctuary, He intercedes with much incense and all the prayers of the saints come up before the mercy seat and the throne of the Father in the form of smoke. Jesus fills the censer with fire and casts it unto the earth.

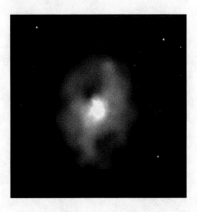

The symbols of this act are witnessed in deep space as the fire of 300 million suns and a mass of smoke greater than all the stars in our galaxy, in our galaxy by the heavens shaking with the flash of energy of 250,000 years of our suns shining in 2/10th of a second, and in our earth by the largest and most devastating earthquake ever recorded.

SHAKING HEAVEN & EARTH

Heaven's bell has rung in our galaxy symbolizing the bells on Christ's robe during the Day of Atonement. The hour of God's judgment has come. But the judgment of God is still mingled with mercy in giving the Holy Spirit.

Joel 2:1 says, "Blow ye the trumpet in Zion, and sound an alarm in my holy mountain: let all the inhabitants of the land tremble: for the day of the LORD cometh, for it is nigh at hand."

Remember what these symbols mean. The fire represents the Holy Spirit that is to turn our hearts back to God again as He did in Elijah's day. Malachi 4:5, 6, "Behold, I will send you Elijah the prophet before the coming of the great and dreadful day of the LORD: 6 And he shall turn the heart of the fathers to the children, and the heart of the children to their fathers, lest I come and smite the earth with a curse." This is the message of Elijah.

The incense represents the intercession and the righteousness of Christ. The Holy Spirit translates our prayers of repentance with groanings that cannot be uttered and the smoke, our translated and holy prayers, ascend before God the Father.

The shaking of the heavens symbolizes the giving of the Holy Spirit for the purpose of giving the glory of Christ, His character of love, His mind. Let this mind be in you which was in Christ Jesus, Philippians 2:5.

The shaking of the earth is a symbol of God revealing His righteous and Holy law. But now He is shaking not only the earth but the heavens, the sea and the dry land, telling us that He is not only the creator but also the re-creator. He is the Author of the new covenant that was ratified by His blood. The shaking of these things is a sign that the Holy Spirit is come to write God's law on our hearts and cause us to obey Him and reflect the glory of Jesus to a dying world. It also symbolizes the judgment by Him who speaks His law from heaven for our God is a consuming fire to sin, which is the transgression of the law.

The conclusion of the whole matter is, "Fear God, and give glory to him; for the hour of his judgment is come: and worship him that made heaven, and earth, and the sea, and the fountains of waters." Revelation 14:7.